Discrete Mathematics and Theoretical Computer Science

T0189545

Springer
London
Berlin
Heidelberg
New York
Barcelona
Hong Kong
Milan
Paris
Singapore
Tokyo

Christof Teuscher

Turing's Connectionism

An Investigation of Neural Network Architectures

Springer

Christof Teuscher, Dipl-Ing EPFL, PhD Candidate (EPFL)
Logic Systems Laboratory, Swiss Federal Institute of Technology Lausanne
(EPFL), EPFL-DI-LSL Ecublens, CH-1015 Lausanne, Switzerland

British Library Cataloguing in Publication Data
Teuscher, Christof
    Turing's connectionism : an investigation of neural
    network architectures. - (Discrete mathematics and
    Theoretical computer science)
    1.Turing, Alan, 1912-1954 2.Neural networks (Computer
    science) 3.Connections (Mathematics)
    I.Title
    006.3'2
    ISBN 1852334754

Library of Congress Cataloging-in-Publication Data
Teuscher, Christof, 1972-
        Turing's connectionism : an investigation of neural network architectures / Christof
        Teuscher.
        p. cm. -- (Discrete mathematics and theoretical computer science, ISSN 14399911)
        Includes bibliographical references and index.
        ISBN 1-85233-475-4 (alk. paper)
        1. Neural networks (Computer science) 2. Turing machines. I. Title. II. Series.
    QA76.87 .T46 2001
    006.3'2--dc21   2001042700

Discrete Mathematics and Theoretical Computer Science Series ISSN 1439-9911
ISBN 1-85233-475-4 Springer-Verlag London Berlin Heidelberg
a member of BertelsmannSpringer Science+Business Media GmbH
http://www.springer.co.uk

Typesetting: Camera ready by author
Printed and bound at the Athenæum Press Ltd., Gateshead, Tyne & Wear
34/3830-54321 Printed on acid-free paper SPIN 10881806

To Ursina

Foreword

Alan Mathison Turing (1912-1954) was the first to carry out substantial research in the field now known as *Artificial Intelligence (AI)*. He was thinking about machine intelligence at least as early as 1941 and during the war circulated a typewritten paper on machine intelligence among his colleagues at the Government Code and Cypher School (GC & CS), Bletchley Park. Now lost, this was undoubtedly the earliest paper in the field of AI. It probably concerned machine learning and heuristic problem-solving; both were topics that Turing discussed extensively during the war years at GC & CS, as was mechanical chess [121].

In 1945, the war in Europe over, Turing was recruited by the National Physical Laboratory (NPL)[1] in London, his brief to design and develop an electronic stored-program digital computer—a concrete form of the universal Turing machine of 1936 [185]. Turing's technical report "Proposed Electronic Calculator"[2], dating from the end of 1945 and containing his design for the *Automatic Computing Engine (ACE)*, was the first relatively complete specification of an electronic stored-program digital computer [193, 197]. (The document "First Draft of a Report on the EDVAC", produced by John von Neumann and the Moore School group at the University of Pennsylvania in May 1945, contained little engineering detail, in particular concerning electronic hardware [202].) Had Turing's ACE been built as he planned, it would have been in a different league from the other early computers, but his colleagues at the NPL thought the engineering work too difficult to attempt and a considerably smaller machine was built. Known as the *Pilot Model ACE*, this machine ran its first program on May 10, 1950. With a clock speed of 1 MHz, it was for some time the fastest computer in the world. Computers deriving from Turing's ACE design remained in use until about 1970 (including the Bendix G-15, arguably the first personal computer). Unfortunately, delays beyond Turing's control resulted in the NPL's losing the race to build the world's first stored-program electronic digital computer—an honour that went to the University of Manchester, where, in Max Newman's Royal So-

---

[1] Digital facsimiles of all NLP documents mentioned in this foreword are available in "The Turing Archive for the History of Computing": http://www.alanturing.net/archive/index/aceindex.html.

[2] A digital facsimile may be viewed in "The Turing Archive for the History of Computing": http://www.alanturing.net/proposed_electronic_calculator.

ciety Computing Machine Laboratory, the "Manchester Baby" ran its first program on June 21, 1948.

In designing the ACE, Artificial Intelligence was not far from Turing's thoughts—he described himself as building "a brain" [21][3]. The otherwise austere "Proposed Electronic Calculator" contained a cameo discussion of computer intelligence and chess:

> "'Can the machine play chess?' It could fairly easily be made to play a rather bad game. It would be bad because chess requires intelligence. We stated at the beginning of this section that the machine should be treated as entirely without intelligence. There are indications however that it is possible to make the machine display intelligence at the risk of its making occasional serious mistakes. By following up this aspect the machine could probably be made to play very good chess" [193, p. 16].

In February 1947, Turing gave a lecture on the ACE to the London Mathematical Society [187]. So far as is known, this was the earliest public lecture to mention computer intelligence, providing a breathtaking glimpse of a new field. Turing discussed the prospect of machines acting intelligently, learning, and beating human opponents at chess, remarking that "[w]hat we want is a machine that can learn from experience" and that "[t]he possibility of letting the machine alter its own instructions provides the mechanism for this".

What is probably Turing's earliest mention to survive of his interest in neural simulation occurs in a letter to the cyberneticist W. Ross Ashby:

> "In working on the ACE I am more interested in the possibility of producing models of the action of the brain than in the practical applications to computing.
>
> The ACE will be used, as you suggest, in the first instance in an entirely disciplined manner, similar to the action of the lower centres, although the reflexes will be extremely complicated. The disciplined action carries with it the disagreeable feature, which you mentioned, that it will be entirely uncritical when anything goes wrong. It will also be necessarily devoid of anything that could be called originality. There is, however, no reason why the machine should always be used in such a manner: there is nothing in its construction which obliges us to do so. It would be quite possible for the machine to try out variations of behaviour and accept or reject them in the manner you describe and I have been hoping to make the machine do this. This is possible because, without altering the design of the machine itself, it

---

[3] The term "Artificial Intelligence" did not come into use until after Turing's death. The first appearance of the term was in 1956, at a conference at Dartmouth College (organised by John McCarthy) entitled "The Dartmouth Summer Research Project on Artificial Intelligence". Turing's original term "machine intelligence" has also persisted, especially in Britain.

can, in theory at any rate, be used as a model of any other machine, by making it remember a suitable set of instructions. The ACE is in fact analogous to the 'universal machine' described in my paper on computable numbers. This theoretical possibility is attainable in practice, in all reasonable cases, at worst at the expense of operating slightly slower than a machine specially designed for the purpose in question. Thus, although the brain may in fact operate by changing its neuron circuits by the growth of axons and dendrites, we could nevertheless make a model, within the ACE, in which this possibility was allowed for, but in which the actual construction of the ACE did not alter, but only the remembered data, describing the mode of behaviour applicable at any time" [184].

By 1947 little progress had been made on the physical construction of the ACE (although much effort had already gone into writing programs or "instruction tables"). The actual engineering work was not being carried out at the NPL but at the Post Office Research Station, under the supervision of Thomas Flowers, who had designed and built *Colossus*, the first fully-functioning large-scale electronic digital computer, installed at Bletchley Park in December 1943. In consequence of his wartime association with Turing, Flowers was asked by the NPL, early in 1946, to assist with the engineering design of, and to build, the ACE. However, the Post Office Research Station was occupied with a backlog of urgent work on the national telephone system (at that time managed by the Post Office) and only two men could be spared to work on the ACE, William Chandler and Allen Coombs (both Chandler and Coombs had played leading roles, on the engineering side, in the wartime Colossus project). As Flowers has said, his Section was "too busy to do other people's work" [58]. In August 1946 Sir Charles Darwin, Director of the NPL, remarked that the Post Office was "not in a position to plunge very deep" and by November was expressing concern to Post Office staff about the slow rate of progress on the ACE [43, 145]. In the middle of 1947, a thoroughly disheartened Turing applied for a twelve-month period of sabbatical leave to be spent in Cambridge. The purpose of the leave, as described by Darwin in July 1947, was to enable Turing

"to extend his work on the machine [ACE] still further towards the biological side. I can best describe it by saying that hitherto the machine has been planned for work equivalent to that of the lower parts of the brain, and he [Turing] wants to see how much a machine can do for the higher ones; for example, could a machine be made that could learn by experience? This will be theoretical work, and better done away from here" [44].

Turing left the NPL for Cambridge in the autumn of 1947[4].

In May 1948 Turing gave up his position at the NPL (breaking what Darwin referred to as "a gentleman's agreement to return here for at least two years after the year's absence") [44]. Work on the ACE had drawn almost to a standstill and an NPL document of April 1948 stated that hardware development was "probably as far advanced 18 months ago" [1]. The fortunes of the ACE finally began to improve later in 1948, following the setting up at the NPL of an Electronics Section under F. M. Colebrook in April 1948. But Turing did not wait. Newman's offer of a job lured a "very fed up" Turing (Robin Gandy's description [70]) to Manchester University, where in May 1948 he was appointed Deputy Director of the Royal Society Computing Machine Laboratory (there being no Director)[5].

In the summer of 1948 Turing completed a report for Darwin describing the outcomes of his research into "how much a machine can do for the higher... parts of the brain"[6]. It was entitled "Intelligent Machinery"[7] (see also [192, 195]). Donald Michie recalls that Turing

"was in a state of some agitation about its reception by his superiors at N.P.L.: 'A bit thin for a year's time off!'" [122].

The headmasterly Darwin—who once complained about the "smudgy" appearance of Turing's work [45]—was, as Turing predicted, displeased with "Intelligent Machinery", describing it as a "schoolboy's essay" and "not suitable for publication" [2, 70]. In reality this far-sighted paper was the first manifesto of Artificial Intelligence; sadly Turing never published it.

"Intelligent Machinery" is a wide-ranging and strikingly original survey of the prospects of AI. In it Turing brilliantly introduced many of the concepts that were later to become central in the field, in some cases after re-invention by others. These included the logic-based approach to problem-solving, now widely used in expert systems, and the idea, subsequently made popular by Newell and Simon, that (as Turing put it) "intellectual activity consists mainly of various kinds of search" [192, p. 23]. Turing anticipated the concept of a genetic algorithm in a brief passage concerning what he calls "genetical or evolutionary search" [192, p. 23] (the term "genetic algorithm" was introduced circa 1975 by John Holland and his research group at the University of Michigan, Ann Arbor). "Intelligent Machinery" also contains the earliest

[4] Probably at the end of September. Turing was still at the NPL when Geoff Hayes arrived in Maths Division on 23 September 1947 [83]. Turing was on half pay during his sabbatical [2].
[5] Turing's salary was paid wholly from a Royal Society grant awarded to Newman for the purpose of developing a stored programme electronic computer [128].
[6] During his sabbatical year Turing also proved that the word problem for semi groups with cancellation is unsolvable [189].
[7] A digital facsimile may be viewed in "The Turing Archive for the History of Computing": http://www.alanturing.net/intelligent_machinery.

description of (a restricted form of) what Turing was later to call the "imitation game" and is now known simply as the *Turing Test* [188]. The major part of "Intelligent Machinery", however, consists of an exquisite discussion of machine learning, in which Turing anticipated the modern approach to AI known as connectionism—the science of computing with networks of artificial neurons.

Modern connectionists regard Donald Hebb and Frank Rosenblatt as the founding figures of their approach and it is not widely realised that Turing wrote a blueprint for much of the connectionist project as early as 1948. In "Intelligent Machinery" he introduced what he called "unorganised machines", giving as examples networks of neuron-like boolean elements connected together in a largely random manner (we call these "Turing Nets"). He described a certain form of Turing Net as "the simplest model of a nervous system" and hypothesised that "the cortex of the infant is an unorganised machine, which can be organised by suitable interfering training". From a historical point of view, his idea that an initially unorganised neural network can be organised by means of "interfering training" is of considerable significance, since it did not appear in the earlier work of McCulloch and Pitts [119]. In Turing's model, the training process renders certain neural pathways effective and others ineffective. He anticipated the modern procedure of simulating, in an ordinary digital computer, neural networks and the process of training them. So far as is known, he was the first person to consider building artificial computing machines out of simple, neuron-like elements connected together into networks in a largely random manner. He claimed a proof (now lost) of the proposition that an initially unorganised Turing Net with sufficient neurons can be organised to become a universal Turing machine with a given storage capacity. This proof first opened up the possibility, noted by Turing, that the human cognitive system is a universal symbol-processor implemented in a neural network.

During his final years Turing worked on (what would now be called) *Artificial Life* or *A-Life*, using the *Manchester Ferranti Mark I* (the first commercially available electronic stored-program computer) to model biological growth [191]. In February 1951 he wrote in a letter to his former assistant at the NPL:

> "Our new machine [the Ferranti Mark I] is to start arriving on Monday. I am hoping as one of the first jobs to do something about 'chemical embryology'. In particular I think one can account for the appearance of Fibonacci numbers in connection with fir-cones" [183].

Turing used the Ferranti Mark I to simulate a chemical mechanism by which the genes of a zygote may determine the anatomical structure of the resulting animal or plant. During this period Turing achieved the distinction of being the first person to engage in the computer-assisted exploration of non-linear dynamical systems (his theory of morphogenesis used non-linear differential equations to express the chemistry of growth).

Turing wrote concerning his work on neural computation and on morphogenesis in a letter to the biologist J. Z. Young:

"I am afraid I am very far from the stage where I feel inclined to start asking any anatomical questions [about the brain]. According to my notions of how to set about it that will not occur until quite a late stage when I have a fairly definite theory about how things are done. At present I am not working on the problem at all, but on my mathematical theory of embryology... This is yielding to treatment, and it will so far as I can see, give satisfactory explanations of i) Gastrulation ii) Polyogonally symmetrical structures, e.g., starfish, flowers iii) Leaf arrangement, in particular the way the Fibonacci series... comes to be involved iv) Colour patterns on animals, e.g., stripes, spots and dappling v) Patterns on nearly spherical structures such as some Radiolaria, but this is more difficult and doubtful. I am really doing this now because it is yielding more easily to treatment. I think it is not altogether unconnected with the other problem. The brain structure has to be one which can be achieved by the genetical embryological mechanism, and I hope that this theory that I am now working on may make clearer what restrictions this really implies. What you tell me about growth of neurons under stimulation is very interesting in this connection. It suggests means by which the neurons might be made to grow so as to form a particular circuit, rather than to reach a particular place" [190].

In the midst of this groundbreaking work Turing died, aged 41.

"One should programme a model with say a few hundred 'neurones' on a computer [and] just see how it does behave" [69]. So wrote the mathematician Robin Gandy, a few months after Turing's death, concerning what he referred to as Turing's "report on learning" ("Intelligent Machinery") and Turing's proposals for neuron-like computation. Unfortunately, Turing Nets were not explored at the time and "Intelligent Machinery" was entirely overlooked. In the year of Turing's death, two researchers at MIT, Wesley Clark and Belmont Farley, succeeded in running the first computer simulations of neural networks. Clark and Farley were unaware of Turing's earlier work and their neural architecture was quite different from his, using weighted connections. Clark and Farley were able to train their networks—which contained a maximum of 128 neurons—to recognise simple patterns [32, 56]. (In addition, they discovered that the random destruction of up to 10% of the neurons in a trained network does not affect the network's performance at its task.) The work begun by Clark and Farley was considerably developed by Frank Rosenblatt, in whose theory of 'perceptrons' modern connectionism took shape [151, 153]. Meanwhile, Turing's pioneering work on a distinctively different type of connectionist architecture was forgotten.

Turing's neural networks of 1948 form the topic of Turing's Connectionism: An Investigation of Neural Network Architectures. So far as we know, after half a century Christof Teuscher is the first to carry out a detailed exploration of Turing Nets[8]. We welcome his investigations of Turing's unorganised machines and look forward to a growth of interest in Turing Nets. As Teuscher amply demonstrates, it is far from true that Turing's ideas are of only historical interest.

July 2001

B. Jack Copeland
Diane Proudfoot

The Turing Project
University of Canterbury
New Zealand

---

[8] Our own earlier investigations, in association with our students Craig Webster, Bruce Webster and Justin Zajec, involved only small numbers of neurons.

Preface

Indispensable qualities for the research worker include independent judgment, intellectual curiosity, perseverance, devotion to country and a burning desire for reputation.
— Santiago Ramón y Cajal, *Advice for a Young Investigator*, 1897.

This book is about Turing's almost forgotten connectionist ideas. What first began as an "ordinary" diploma thesis [177] (equivalent to a Master's thesis) at the *Logic Systems Laboratory (LSL)*[9], *Swiss Federal Institute of Technology Lausanne (EPFL)*[10] to obtain a degree in computer engineering finally ended up as a book after more than one year of additional research and hard work!

It was in April 1999 that the *Scientific American* journal published an article by B. Jack Copeland and Diane Proudfoot on Turing's forgotten ideas in computer science [40]. An important part of the paper was dedicated to Turing's connectionist models, called *unorganized machines*, the rest to *hypercomputation*, i.e., computation beyond the Turing limit. I read this article with great interest and was immediately fascinated by Turing's very simple neural-network-like machines. At the same time, several fundamental questions arose and I felt that a lot of investigations could still be done around Turing's unorganized machines.

Copeland and Proudfoot's work not only inspired this book but also served as a theoretical foundation besides Turing's writings.

The initial report—entitled "Study, Implementation, and Evolution of the Artificial Neural Networks Proposed by Alan M. Turing. A Revival of his 'Schoolboy' Ideas" [177]—has been available on the web since April 2000. To my big surprise, many people from all over the world became interested in the work. Jack Copeland, whom I first met during a hypercomputation workshop in London in May 2000, strongly encouraged me to publish the initial report in the form of a book.

The resulting book is—as its title says—strongly focused on Turing's connectionism. The book is *not* about Turing's entire and undoubtedly very rich

---

[9] http://lslwww.epfl.ch
[10] http://www.epfl.ch

lifework. This work has a clear basis in Turing's initial "Intelligent Machinery" paper, however, many topics significantly depart from Turing's original ideas. I have always tried to clearly state what came from Turing and what has been extended or newly invented by others or by myself. The book presents an in-depth analysis of Turing's connectionist ideas from today's point of view and thus also tries to answer some questions that Turing himself did not think of. An example is the interconnectivity of his networks: Why does each node only have two incoming links? Would networks with more inputs not perform better? An answer shall be given thanks to recent investigations in the domain of random boolean networks.

The goal of this book was not only to investigate Turing's initial ideas but also to finish off some of his thoughts. Thus, his dream of applying some sort of "genetical search" to organize his unorganized machines has become reality. The investigation of his networks from the complex-systems-theory point of view made a bridge between his connectionist ideas and his work on morphogenesis which formed the basis for the modern non-linear dynamical systems theory.

Undoubtedly, most of the modern connectionist approaches are a great deal more complex and complicated than Turing's models. This is not to say that modern approaches are more powerful in general, on the contrary. The boolean approach is still very attractive for any implementation of neural networks in hardware. Furthermore, many a researcher is still convinced that, despite the extreme complexity of the human brain, its essential functions can be mimicked by boolean models. However, even among specialists, the opinions are largely divided. Anyway, it is not in the scope of this book to judge on that question. I hope to have provided rather "neutral" facts rather than personal and biased opinions.

To the best of my knowledge, B. Jack Copeland, Diane Proudfoot, and their former students Craig Webster[11], Bruce Webster and Justin Zajec are the only persons who also investigated Turing's unorganized machines.

The work on Turing's connectionism presented in this book has been honoured by the following awards:

- *Annaheim Foundation Award*, April 2000. Awards an excellent bio-inspired thesis.
- *Jean Landry Award*, April 2000. Awards an original and personal scientific work.
- *Asea Brown Bovery (ABB) Research Award Switzerland*, September 2000.

I have tried to open the scope of the book as wide as possible. There are topics for almost any kind of reader interested in Turing and in his connectionist ideas. A priori, no special knowledge is required to read this book. Some sections are rather technical, but may be skipped without missing the

---

[11] Craig Webster maintains his own web-site about Turing's connectionism: http://home.clear.net.nz/pages/cw.

global message. The book starts from Turing's initial ideas and diverges more and more towards new ideas and related topics. It was impossible to provide an in-depth analysis of all topics, however, by means of the literature referenced, it should not be too much of a problem for the interested reader to probe further.

Turing's work is not always easy to read and it is often possible to interpret it in different ways. I really hope not to have misinterpreted any of his thoughts.

Finally, I would be grateful for comments, reviews, corrections, links, news, etc. from readers sent to me at christof@teuscher.ch. Everything will also be made available on the book's web-site (see Section 1.6).

Lausanne, May 2001   *Christof Teuscher*
                                                  christof@teuscher.ch
                                            http://www.teuscher.ch/christof

Acknowledgments

The essence of science: ask a impertinent question,
and you are on the way to a pertinent answer.
— Jacob Bronowski, *The Ascent of Man*, 1973.

In developing and writing this book I have benefited from a great deal of help of various kinds. This work would certainly not have been possible without the support and the direct or indirect influence of many people. I am very grateful to all the friends, families, and colleagues who either have read previous portions of the manuscript or have contributed to it through many thoughtful discussions.

First, of course, I am extremely grateful to my wife Ursina, who has for far too long put up with me spending evenings and weekends in front of our computers. I am very grateful to her for having uncompromisingly supported me every day!

I have only the deepest thanks for my parents and my family who supported me whenever possible and made considerable sacrifices in order to give me all possible advantages in life and during my studies.

I am very grateful to B. Jack Copeland, who strongly encouraged me to write this book and reviewed the initial manuscript very carefully. Many contributions and valuable comments helped to greatly improve the manuscript. Many thanks also, Jack and Diane, for having accepted to write the foreword!

Very special thanks go to Andrew Hodges for the review of the manuscript, his comments, and his interest in my work.

Many a student directly or indirectly contributed to this book with experiments. I would especially like to thank to Olivier Bruchez, Christophe Krebser, Camille Weber, and Richard Greset for their work!

I am grateful to Eduardo Sanchez, to Jacques Zahnd, to Daniel Mange, and to Pierre Marchal for their help, comments and suggestions. Many thanks, Eduardo, for having supervised my diploma thesis and for all the discussions! A special thanks goes to Carlos Andrés Peña Reyes for his advice with MATLAB.

I am indebted to the *Springer-Verlag* editor Rebecca Mowat and to the *Discrete Mathematics and Computer Science Series* editor Cristian S. Calude for their suggestions and their help that made this book possible.

I thank all members of the *Logic Systems Laboratory* for making the past a thoroughly enjoyable and rewarding experience! A special thanks goes to "Chico", alias André Badertscher, master of plays on words and heroic guardian of the laboratory, its members and equipment.

For all people who were not mentioned individually and supported this work with helpful suggestions.

Contents

1. Introduction

Turing believes machines think
Turing lies with men
Therefore machines do not think.
— Alan Turing in a letter to Norman Routledge, 1952 (see also preface of
Alan Turing: The Enigma [91]).

1.1 Turing's Anticipation of Connectionism

It was in 1948 that Alan Turing wrote a little-known report entitled "Intelligent Machinery" [192, 195]. At that time, he was employed at the National Physical Laboratory (NPL) in London where he worked on the design of an electronic computer—the *Automatic Computing Engine (ACE)*. Turing never had great interest in publicizing his ideas, so the paper went unpublished until 1968, 14 years after his death. The report first appeared in an edited collection by Evans and Robertson [55] in 1968 and the following year in the journal *Machine Intelligence* [192].

Few people know that the "Intelligent Machinery" paper contains a fascinating investigation of different connectionist models that would today be called *neural networks*. It is amazing that his employer at the National Physical Laboratory, Sir Charles Darwin, grandson of the well-known English naturalist, dismissed the manuscript as a "schoolboy essay" [2, 70] (see also foreword). In describing networks of artificial neurons connected in a random manner, Turing has written one of the first manifests of the field of *artificial intelligence* (although he did not use this term). One of the questions he was always interested in was whether it is possible for machinery to show intelligent behaviour or not. Copeland and Proudfoot write:

> "Turing was probably the first person to consider building computing machines out of simple, neuron-like elements connected together into networks in a largely random manner" [39].

His 1948 paper pioneered in fact many of the ideas presented in his famous philosophical *Mind* paper of 1950 [188]. Turing always favoured the connectionist as well as the classical programming approach to artificial intelligence. With the failure of classical artificial intelligence, there has been more willingness in recent years to combine both approaches into hybrid systems.

Two recent publications by B. Jack Copeland and Diane Proudfoot in the *Scientific American* [40] and in the *Synthese* journal [39] revived Turing's anticipated neural-network-like machines and showed new analyzes. Copeland and Proudfoot are the directors of *The Turing Archive for the History of Computing* [182] at the University of Canterbury, an ongoing project around Turing's lifework. Computational investigation of Turing's neural network architectures is one of their research topics.

Turing himself called his networks *unorganized machines*. He basically proposed three types of machines: A-type, B-type, and P-type unorganized machines. A-type and B-type machines are boolean networks made up of extremely simple, randomly interconnected neurons (NAND gates), each having exactly two inputs. The neurons are synchronized by means of a global clock signal. In comparison to A-type networks, Turing's B-type networks have modifiable interconnections (basically a switch) and thus, an external agent can "organize" these machines—by enabling and disabling the connections—to perform a required job. Turing's idea behind the introduction of his B-type networks was to open the possibility of reinforcing successful and useful links and of cutting useless ones. His deeper motivation was to build structures which allow for learning. On the other hand, the idea of organizing an initially random network of neurons and connections is undoubtedly one of the most significant aspects of Turing's "Intelligent Machinery" paper.

Turing, always concerned with universal computation, wrote:

> "[...] that with suitable initial conditions they [i.e., B-type machines] will do any required job, given sufficient time and provided the number of units is sufficient. In particular with a B-type unorganized machine with sufficient units one can find initial conditions which will make it into a universal machine with a given storage capacity" [192, p. 15].

The third type of machine—the P-type machine—is not really a connectionist machine but a modified Turing machine without a tape that has two additional inputs: the *pleasure input* and the *pain input*. The idea is that, initially, the machine is largely incomplete and that the application of "pleasure" and "punishment" stimuli by an external teacher completes the internal tables. P-type machines shall very briefly be described in this book too, although they are not connectionist models.

Few people realize that Turing was one of the first to propose a sort of genetic algorithm—called *genetical* or *evolutionary search*—to train his unorganized machines:

"There is the genetical or evolutionary search by which a combination of genes is looked for, the criterion being survival value. The remarkable success of this search confirms to some extent the idea that intellectual activity consists mainly of various kinds of search" [192, p. 23].

At that time, Turing was naturally unable to apply genetical search to the optimization of his unorganized machines because of missing computing resources and computing power. The very same approach will, however, be investigated in detail in this book.

It is interesting that Turing makes absolutely no reference to the groundbreaking work of McCulloch and Pitts [119], published in 1943. Copeland and Proudfoot write:

"Turing had undoubtedly heard something of the work of McCulloch and Pitts. [...] Turing and McCulloch seem not to have met until 1949. After their meeting Turing spoke dissmissively of McCulloch, referring to him as a charlatan. It is an open question whether the work of McCulloch and Pitts had any influence whatsoever on the development of the ideas presented in the 1948 report" [39, p. 372].

McCulloch and Pitts' work was, in fact, itself influenced by Turing's 1937 paper [185].

"Their 1943 article represents the first attempt to apply what they refer to as 'the Turing definition of computability' to the study of neuronal function [119, p. 129]. McCulloch stressed the extent to which his and Pitts' work is indebted to Turing in the course of some autobiographical remarks made during the public discussion of a lecture given by von Neumann in 1948" [39, p. 371].

McCulloch's words were cited by von Neumann as follows:

"I started entirely in the wrong angle...and it was not until I saw Turing's paper [185] that I began to get going the right way around, and with Pitts' help formulated the required logical calculus. What we thought we were doing (and I think we succeeded fairly well) was treating the brain as a Turing machine" [204, p. 319].

McCulloch and Pitts' boolean neurons are slightly more complex than Turing's neurons. They can have as many inputs as they like and provide inhibitory and exhibitory synapses. Like Turing's model, they make, however, no use of weighted connections. Turing's networks and McCulloch and Pitts' neurons are thus equivalent in the extended sense, as it shall be shown in Section 5.4.

In 1950, Turing became very interested in the theory of growth and form in biology, a topic he called the mathematical theory of *morphogenesis* (see

Collected Works of A. M. Turing: Morphogenesis [158]). His interest included naturally the idea of how brains grow new connections and how biological structures, so complex and beautiful (e.g., symmetry in nature, etc.), emerge from the viewpoint of nonlinear physics and chemistry. Already in his childhood he had been spotted and sketched "watching the daisies grow" [91]. The interest in natural growth processes was an astonishing change of direction in his studies, but might be seen as a return to a fundamental problem already encountered in his childhood.

The growth of new connections within the brain is naturally closely related to Turing's connectionist ideas of 1948. His first paper on morphogenesis [191]—overlooked for a long time—became then a founding paper of modern non-linear dynamical theory. The recent investigations of the dynamical behaviour of Turing's neural networks presented in this book thus make a bridge between his morphogenesis work and his connectionist ideas.

Turing's work about neuron-like computation and morphogenesis shows that he preferred to follow his own path. Kleene wrote: "It was, perhaps, a defect of his qualities that he found it hard to accept the work of others, preferring to work things out himself" [103, p. 492]. Nevertheless, there is certainly no doubt that Turing was one of the most important 20th-century mathematicians and that he was among the first to imagine the possibility of machines—includes his connectionist machines—that really think.

1.2 Alan Mathison Turing

As this work is largely inspired by Turing, a short biography of this remarkable man should not be missing. (Note that the foreword also contains many pertinent information.) Extensive information about Turing's life can be found on Andrew Hodges Turing home page [181] and in his excellent and beautifully written Turing biographies [90–92]. Copeland and Proudfoot also maintain a site about Turing [182]. Further links to web-sites can be found in Chapter 6.

Various books and collections of Turing's work are also available. The interested reader is referred to Ince [95] (collection), Millican and Clark [124], Clark and Millican [31], Herken [86], Saunders [158] (collection), and Britton [25] (collection).

Alan Mathison Turing was born in London on June 23, 1912 as the son of Julius Mathison and Ethel Sara Turing.

Early in his childhood, Alan Turing began to show an extraordinary aptitude for science and mathematics. In 1931, he entered King's College in Cambridge. At the end of the third year he had already gained a distinction and in 1935, he was elected a Fellow of King's for a dissertation on the "Central Limit Theorem of Probability". In the same year, he became interested in mathematical logic. This made him one of the great pioneers of the computer field and laid the theoretical groundwork for modern computing science (along with others, including Church, Post, Kleene, Gödel, etc.). The concept of the *Turing machine* was published by Turing in 1936 in his now celebrated paper "On Computable Numbers with an Application to the Entscheidungsproblem" [185]. The concept of the Turing machine was revolutionary for the time where most computers were designed for a particular purpose or a limited range of purposes only. What Turing envisioned was a machine that could do anything, something that we take for granted today: the *universal Turing machine*. The method of instructing the computer was very important in Turing's concept. He essentially described a machine which knew a few simple instructions. Making the computer perform a particular task was simply a matter of breaking the job down into a series of these simple instructions. This is identical to the process programmers go through today. The hard part was determining what the simple steps were and how to break down the larger problems.

Turing's paper led to an invitation to Princeton, where he worked with Alonzo Church, who also supervised his Ph.D. thesis. In 1938 he completed his thesis entitled "Systems of Logic Based on Ordinals" which was subsequently published in 1939 [186]. Turing was offered a post as assistant to John von Neumann, but decided to return to Cambridge where he worked on the Zeta function.

During the Second World War, Turing worked as chief cryptanalyst at the *Government Code and Cypher School*, Bletchley Park, the centre of the British code-breaking work during the war. Turing's principal role was that of cracking the code of the German *Enigma* cipher machine. The work was kept confidential for many years.

In 1945, he joined the Mathematics Divison at the *National Physical Laboratory (NPL)* where he worked on the design of an electronic computer—the *Automatic Computing Engine (ACE)*. In a little-known paper—a report for the NPL—entitled "Intelligent Machinery" [192,195], Turing investigated connectionist networks. But he never had great interest in publicizing his ideas, so the paper went unpublished until 1968 [55]. He left the NPL in 1948.

Turing was then appointed a Readership at Manchester University, where he continued his work on the Zeta function, on computing machines, intelligence, and on morphogenesis. Turing believed that machines could be created that would mimic the processes of the human brain. He discussed the possibility of such machines, acknowledging the difficulty people would have accepting a machine that would rival their own intelligence, a problem that still plagues artificial intelligence today. In his mind, there was nothing the brain could do that a well designed computer could not.

Turing died on June 7 1954 of cyanide poisoning.

1.3 Connectionism and Artificial Neural Networks

This section shall give a very brief overview on artificial neural networks and connectionism.

From the viewpoint of neural network research, *connectionism* [34] is a movement in cognitive science which hopes to explain human intellectual abilities using artificial neural networks.

> "There is considerable diversity among connectionist models, but all models are built up of the same basic components: simple processing elements and weighted connections between those elements" [54].

Connectionism has a very long past. One can trace the origin of connectionist ideas to the early Greek philosopher, Aristotle, and his ideas on mental associations. However, the birth date and opening shot in neural network research was the 1943 paper by McCulloch and Pitts [119]. They proved that any logical expression could be implemented by an appropriate net of simplified neurons. They assumed that each neuron was binary and had a finite threshold, that each synapse was either excitory or inhibitory and caused a finite delay of one cycle, and that the networks could be constructed with multiple synapses between any pair of nodes.

Artificial neural networks (ANN) have been inspired by the recognition that the human brain processes information in an entirely different way from the classical von Neumann digital computer. The human brain is a highly complex, parallel, and nonlinear information processing machine made up of about 10^{11} neurons whereas each neuron is connected to 10^3 to 10^4 other neurons. The information is stored in the contact points between different neurons, the *synapses*.

An artificial neural network is an information processing system which is made up of a number of simple, highly interconnected processing elements—the *neurons*—which process information in parallel. As a simplification, the neuron might be considered as a sort of *detector* that detects the existence of some set of conditions and that responds with a signal that communicates the extent to which those conditions have been met [136]. Artificial neural networks can be considered as an alternative approach to the problem of computation just as biological neural networks are one of many possible solutions to the problem of processing information. Most often, artificial neural networks are "neural" only in the sense that they have been inspired by *neuroscience* but not necessarily because they are faithful models of biologic neural and cognitive phenomena. For example, connectionists usually do not attempt to explicitly model the variety of different kinds of brain neurons, nor the effects of neurotransmitters and hormones. Even today, connectionist networks are designed most often by hand and reflect important theoretical claims, experience, and knowledge on the part of the modeller. There are very little general rules on how to design connectionist models. The network's architecture and topology is often the most important part. Elman stated: "[...] part of what a network knows lies in its architecture" [54]. Nevertheless, artificial neural networks are a broadly accepted and viable computational model for a wide variety of problems.

Figure 1.1 shows the structure of an abstract neuron [150]. Each input has an associated weight. The input value x_i is usually multiplied by the weight w_i. The neuron's output is computed with a *primitive function* that can be selected arbitrarily. Thus, "[...] artificial neural networks are nothing but *networks of primitive functions*" [150]. Many different neuron models, primitive functions, network topologies, timing characteristics, etc. have been proposed since the model of McCulloch and Pitts [119] and Turing's unorganized machines.

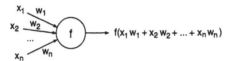

Fig. 1.1. An abstract neuron. Each input has an associated weight. The input value x_i is usually multiplied by the weight w_i. The neuron's output is computed with a function that can be selected arbitrarily.

Learning is the ability of the brain to adapt its behaviour to a changing environment. Normally, this ability is used to improve the performance of the system, e.g., of a human being or animal in its environment. As Simon Haykin stated, "the process of learning is a matter of viewpoint, which makes it all the more difficult to agree on a precise definition of the term" [84]. For example, learning viewed by a psychologist is quite different from learning in a classroom sense. In this book, only the following definition of learning is considered:

Definition 1.3.1 (Learning in the context of neural networks)
Learning is a process by which the free parameters of a neural network are adapted through a process of stimulation by the environment in which the network is embedded. The type of learning is determined by the manner in which the parameter changes take place [84, p. 50]. ∎

Learning in artificial neural networks can be regarded as a search for parameters (weights, thresholds, switches, etc.) that optimize a predefined function (input-output mapping). Learning in artificial neural networks is hard and requires exponential time irrespective of the learning algorithm used. Judd [96, 97] showed that the learning problem in neural networks is NP-complete, even for approximative learning. Thus, in the worst case, one will not be able to do much better than just randomly exhausting all combinations of settings to see if one happens to work. However, these theoretical results do not rule out the possibility of finding a polynomial-time algorithm for the training of certain classes of problems [82].

Learning algorithms can be classified into two main classes (see also Figure 1.2) [150]:

- *supervised learning*
- *unsupervised learning*

The basic difference between these two learning modes concerns whether the net uses an external report (from the supervisor) to modify its performance. Supervised learning basically relies on three things [30]:

1. input,
2. the net's internal dynamics, and
3. an evaluation of its weight-setting job.

On the other hand, unsupervised learning relies on two things only:

1. input, and
2. the dynamics of the net.

No external report on its behaviour vis-a-vis its weight-setting progress is provided.

> "In either case, the point of the learning algorithm is to produce a weight configuration that can be said to represent something in the world, in the sense that when activated by an input vector, the correct answer is produced" [30].

Unsupervised learning is normally used when, for a given input, the exact output the network should produce is unknown. Supervised learning is further divided into methods which use *reinforcement learning* or *error correction*. Reinforcement learning is used when after each presentation of an input-output example we only know whether the network produces the desired result or not. The weights are updated based on this information (that is, the boolean values *true* or *false*) so that only the input vector can be used for weight correction. In learning with error correction, the magnitude of an error, together with the input vector, determines the magnitude of the correction to the weights.

One of the simplest learning rules that can be used is *Hebbian learning*, proposed in 1949 by the psychologist Donald Hebb [85]. His idea was that two neurons which are simultaneously active should develop a degree of interaction higher than those neurons whose activities are uncorrelated [150]. During learning both input and output are clamped to the network and the weight update is given by:

$$\Delta w_{ij} = \eta x_i x_j \qquad \text{The Hebb rule} \tag{1.1}$$

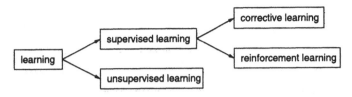

Fig. 1.2. Classes of learning algorithms.

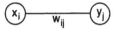

Fig. 1.3. Illustration of the Hebb rule.

The factor η is the learning constant. Figure 1.3 illustrates the Hebb rule. This rule is also referred to as *Hebbian plasticity*. Hebb gave this formulation in 1949:

> "When an axon of cell A is near enough to excite cell B and repeatedly or persistently takes part in firing it, some growth process or metabolic change takes place in one or both cells such that A's efficiency, as one of the cells firing B, is increased" [85].

As a consequence, the increase in strength in some synapses must be compensated for by a decrease in others. Only the more successful synapses can grow; the less successful ones weaken and eventually disappear [201].

One synapse on its own cannot efficiently produce favourable events. For that it needs the cooperation of other synapses. The rules of cooperation and competition act on a local scale and are able to produce ordered connection patterns. However, they do not necessarily organize the nervous system for optimal biological utility [201]. Malsburg also concluded that central control as the only criterion for growth or decay of synapses is not sufficient. This is simply a problem of scale. A central controller would not have enough time to regulate the strength of all the synapses of the human cerebral cortex.

Reinforcement learning is learning what do to, i.e., learning how to map situations to actions, so as to maximize a numerical reward signal. The learner is not told which actions to take, as in most forms of machine learning, but instead must discover which actions yield the most reward by trying them. Reinforcement learning is thus defined not by characterizing learning methods, but by characterizing a learning problem [174]. Reinforcement learning is different from supervised learning, the kind of learning studied in most current research in machine learning and artificial neural networks. Supervised learning is learning from examples provided by a knowledgeable external supervisor. However, it is not always possible to obtain examples of a desired behaviour that are both correct and representative for all situations in which the system has to act. For further reading about reinforcement learning, I highly recommend Sutton and Barto [174].

A wide variety of neural network literature is available and every year an enormous amount of papers is published in international journals and on conferences. Rojas' book [150] is a good introduction for beginners whereas Haykin [84] offers an excellent and comprehensive foundation for the mathematically interested expert. Arbib's "Handbook of Brain Theory and Neural Networks" [10] offers an excellent encyclopedic collection of papers that cover almost every domain in neural network research and brain-level theories. For readers interested in cognitive neuroscience and biologically inspired neural networks, a good starting point might be O'Reilly and Munakata's book [136] or Churchland's "The Computational Brain" [30].

1.4 Historical Context and Related Work

This section shall provide a list of related work that is of some historical interest, but shall also mention related work that influenced connectionists to this very day. Note, that Copeland and Proudfoot provide in [39] a comprehensive summary on early work on neuron-like computation.

The idea of using simple neurons was not really new at Turing's time. Like Turing, already McCulloch and Pitts considered in 1943 boolean networks of very simple two-state neurons without the use of weighted connections or variable thresholds [119]. With regard to McCulloch and Pitts, there is however no doubt, that Turing's work on neural networks goes importantly beyond the earlier work of McCulloch and Pitts [39]. Turing's idea of using supervised interference in form of an evolutionary algorithm to train an initially random arrangement of units to compute a specified function was certainly new and revolutionary for that time.

It should also be mentioned that the *cybernetics* movement and the interest in *self-organizing systems* certainly had an influence on the connectionist movement and vice versa. Important contributions came from Wiener [215] and Asbhy [11,13], but also from McCulloch. Wiener defines cybernetics to be "the science of control and communication in the animal and the machine". The word cybernetics is derived from the Greek *cybernetes*, which means steersman. The cyberneticists wondered if they could make a *thinking machine*, a machine that would be an electrical imitation of the human nervous system. One of their investigations was the creation of the concept of feedback.

In the early fifties, computers, psychology, and philosophy for the first time try to join together. On the one hand, *cognitivism* tried to model the human mind whereas *connectionism* tried to model the human brain. It was Wesley Clark and Belmont Farley and not Hebb who first simulated in 1954 an artificial neural network [32,56]. In 1956, Rosenblatt unveiled his neuron—the *perceptron*—that was principally based on Hebb's ideas [85]. Hebb suggested that a mass of neurons could learn if their connection-strengths change according to some rule—today known as the *Hebbian rule* (see also Section 1.3).

Towards the end of the sixties, the proofs on the limitations of simple perceptrons by Minsky and Papert [125] nearly caused the complete abandonment of connectionism. Minsky and Papert [126] further developed the perceptron based on the foundations laid by Rosenblatt [152, 153].

In 1956, Allanson published a paper on randomly connected neural networks [7]. The neurons he used were simple, but more complex than McCulloch-Pitts elements. He concluded the paper with the following statement:

> "The behaviour of the most elementary networks, assuming neurons to be far more simple than they are in reality, is more varied and complex than has normally been assumed" [7].

One of the earliest attempts to classify patterns by machine came from Olivier Selfridge [160, 161] in 1958. Courageous, he stated: "Can a machine think? The answer is certainly: yes". Selfridge contributed a significant model called *Pandemonium* for parallel processing, a model that was able to learn to classify patterns.

Large random logical nets made up from McCulloch-Pitts formal threshold neurons have also been investigated in 1962 by Smith and Davidson [170] and by Asbhy et al. [12].

Rozonoér [154] published a paper on random logical nets in 1968 (originally written in Russian). He analyzed the properties of logical random nets consisting of elements whose properties depend on parameters chosen at random. The connections among the elements were also chosen at random. Rozonoér suggested that:

> "[...] objects of this type may present a certain interest in connection with physiological models and, possibly, will have direct technical applications in the future" [154].

In 1971, Amari [8] published a paper on the characteristics of randomly connected threshold-element networks with the intention of understanding some aspects of information processing in nervous systems. He showed that two statistical parameters are sufficient to determine the characteristics of networks. In his 1972 paper [9], Amari further investigated the stability of state transitions in logical nets of threshold elements. For example, he showed that a net reaches an equilibrium state within k state transitions if its initial state is located within a distance of the kth stability number from the equilibrium state (in the sense of the Hamming distance).

Aleksander et al. [6] have developed a pattern recognition system—called *WISARD*—based on a network without feedback made up of boolean processing elements, that was later further developed [4]. The WISARD machine consists of a set of n-input boolean functions whose outputs are summed up.

The key observation is that a boolean function may be implemented as a lock-up table in RAM. Aleksander also investigated the stability of randomly interconnected boolean networks [3].

Fukushima's *Cognitron* [64] and *Neocognitron* [65, 66] laid another milestone for systems based on threshold units. Compared to the WISARD system, Fukushima used feedback connections in his networks.

Martland [115] showed that it is possible to predict the activity of a boolean network with randomly connected inputs, if the characteristics of the boolean neurons can be described probabilistically. In a second paper [114], Martland illustrated how the boolean networks are used to store and retrieve patterns and even pattern sequences auto-associatively. He used networks with feedback connections and neurons similar to Aleksander's WISARD neurons. The synchronously operating networks can work in two modes: (1) running mode and (2) training mode. Martland contributed further work about the behaviour of boolean networks: [116, 117].

Crayton C. Walker was one of the first persons to investigate the effect of the system size on the behaviour of complex systems, namely networks made up from elements that compute recursive logical functions of two binary inputs and two internal states [207]. Later, he also investigated attractors of sparsely connected boolean networks [208].

Very little work has been done around asynchronous random networks of threshold elements. Harvey and Bossomaier [80] have shown that they behave radically different from the deterministic synchronous version. Earlier, Grondin et al. investigated the asynchronous behaviour of threshold-element networks and the role of deterministic chaos [76]. More recent work about rhythmic and non-rhythmic attractors in asynchronous random boolean networks comes from Di Paolo [137, 138].

Important contributions around random boolean networks, their characteristics and dynamics came from Stuart Kauffman [98–101] and Weisbuch [212, 213].

In the domain of language acquisition, James Hurford published a paper entitled "Random Boolean Nets and Features of Language" [94]. He uses the framework of Kauffman's random boolean networks to cast several properties of natural languages: complexity, interconnectedness, stability, diversity, and undeterminedness. Thereby, a given language is modeled as an attractor of the network.

The Ph.D. thesis of E. Mayoraz investigates feedforward boolean neural networks with discrete weights [118]. Different learning algorithms and the computational power is investigated.

For hardware implementations of boolean neural networks and simulated annealing optimization, one might take a look at Niittylahti [129–132].

1.5 Organization of the Book

This book starts from Turing's initial ideas described in his "Intelligent Machinery" paper, but significantly departs from them. Because of a silly mistake in the definition of one of his machines, new types of machines became quickly necessary. Many interesting topics that have not even been mentioned by Turing are discussed in this book (i.e., complex dynamics, attractors, etc.).

Chapter 2 starts with a general introduction of the most important machines invented by Turing. Especially, the Turing and the universal Turing machines shall be briefly presented in Section 2.1.2 and Section 2.1.3. The P-type machine, a Turing machine without tape that can be "organized" is briefly described in Section 2.1.5.

Section 2.2 gives a detailed overview on the unorganized machines presented in Turing's "Intelligent Machinery" paper. The machines are then mathematically formalized and analyzed in Section 2.3. This section also contains some examples, but might be skipped without loosing the global message. It is then shown in Section 2.3.6 that certain unorganized machines that Turing proposed are not universal, i.e., that they cannot compute every logical function. Based on that discovery, new unorganized machines shall be introduced in Section 2.4. At the end of Chapter 2, a very simple MATLAB toolbox is presented that allows the readers to start their own experiments with Turing's unorganized machines.

Figure 1.4 shows an overview on the different network types described in this book. The A-type network—proposed by Turing himself—is the ancestor of all other networks. The networks are further divided into networks allowing interference (i.e., networks that allow to enable and disable links) and networks that do not.

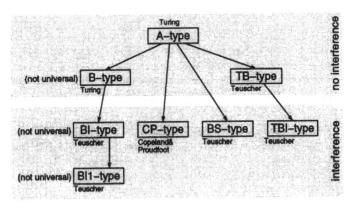

Fig. 1.4. Overview on the different network types described in this book.

Chapter 3 demonstrates how logical functions and digital systems can be realized by means of unorganized networks. This chapter does not yet deal with the "organization" of the machines. All networks used are designed by hand and for a particular task. Several components that might be used to implement a real-world Turing machine are realized by means of unorganized machines. The realization of a Turing machine comes thus within reach and essentially remains an engineering problem. The principal goal of such an implementation is to illustrate the universality of unorganized machines.

Chapter 3 ends with a section about the hardware implementation of unorganized machines. It is shown that Turing's networks can very efficiently be implemented in hardware, especially reconfigurable circuits, so called *Field Programmable Gate Arrays (FPGA)*. A hardware implementation is principally interesting because of the speed-up that can be achieved.

The "organization" of unorganized machines is an important issue that is addressed in detail in this book. Turing himself already dreamed of organizing his machines by means of a sort of genetic algorithm. Chapter 4 makes this dream a reality. Different examples, mainly pattern classification tasks, illustrate the capabilities of unorganized machines. Encoding techniques as well as signal processing are also addressed. Section 4.7 presents a simulated annealing learning algorithm for Turing's neural networks.

Unorganized machines are complex dynamical systems that possess very interesting characteristics. Chapter 5 shall give an overview on different network properties and complex dynamics. The computational power is investigated in Section 5.2 and it is shown that any logical function can be realized by means of the universal unorganized networks. It is also shown that threshold logic and Turing networks are equivalent in the extended sense. The complex dynamics of unorganized machines are best analyzed within a state-space model. This approach is briefly presented in Section 5.5.

Stuart Kauffman's random boolean networks (RBN) are very close relatives to Turing's networks. It is shown in Section 5.6 that unorganized machines are a subset of RBNs and that they exhibit many similar properties. Network activity, network stability, attractors, chaos, and bifurcation are also investigated in Chapter 5. Section 5.10 presents a self-organizing topology evolving algorithm that self-organizes the networks interconnectivity towards a critical value of $K = 2$ for large networks. The most interesting behaviour of unorganized machines occurs in $K = 2$ networks, an interconnectivity value that Turing himself chose.

The question whether unorganized machines can compute beyond the Turing limit is discussed in Section 5.11. A general overview on hypercomputation is also given.

A short epilogue terminates the book in Chapter 6.

1.6 Book Web-Site

The readers of this book are invited to visit the book's own web-site at:

```
http://www.teuscher.ch/turing
```

The web-site contains corrections of this book, readers' comments, readers' contributions, all programming resources presented in this book, further contributions, useful links, and much more.

2. Intelligent Machinery

We are not interested in the fact that the brain
has the consistency of cold porridge.
— Alan M. Turing, "Can automatic calculating machines be said to think?"
Discussion transmitted on BBC Third Programme, 1952 (Transcript [196]).

"Someday, perhaps soon, we will build a machine that will be able to perform the functions of a human mind, a thinking machine" [88], the first sentence in Hillis' book on the *Connection Machine*, a legendary computing machine that provided a large number of tiny processors and memory cells connected by a programmable communications network. Alan Turing probably had a very similar vision much earlier in the 20th century. What was real processor and real memory for Hillis was pencil and paper for Turing.

In his work, Alan M. Turing described various types of machines—some well-known today, others almost forgotten. One of the best known, yet abstract machine invented by Turing is certainly the classical Turing machine [185]. Turing's lifelong interest in thinking machines and his concerns in modelling the human mind by machines (see for example [71, 168]) were probably at the origin of his rather little known paper on mechanical intelligence, a report for the National Physical Laboratory entitled "Intelligent Machinery" [192, 195]:

"I propose to investigate the question as to whether it is possible
for machinery to show intelligent behaviour" [192, p. 3].

The design of intelligent machines is a subject that has interested philosophers and researchers for a very long time. Today, many a philosopher and humanist thinker is convinced that the quest for *artificial intelligence (AI)* or *machine intelligence* has turned out to be a failure. Some eminent critics have even argued that a truly intelligent machine cannot be constructed. But what is intelligence and what can intelligent machines do? To most observers, the essence of intelligence is cleverness, a versatility in solving novel problems [27]. Others even tried to count the number of intelligences [72]. Anyway, it definitely seems that we shall never agree on a universal definition of intelligence because it is an open-ended word. Psychology, philosophy, linguistics, and computer science offer various perspectives and methodologies for studying intelligence.

So what are intelligent machines able to do? In AI for example, computers are programmed to yield "intelligent" behaviour without necessarily attempting to provide a correlation between structures in the program and structures of the brain. On the other hand, *neural computation* develops new strategies for building "intelligent" machines or adaptive robots. However, the final design usually departs radically from the biological neural network that inspired it. Neural networks are "neural" only in the sense that they have been inspired by neuroscience but not necessarily because they are faithful models of biological neural and cognitive phenomena. Nevertheless, they are a viable computational model for a wide variety of problems.

2.1 Machines

"It will not be possible to discuss possible means of producing intelligent machinery without introducing a number of technical terms to describe different kinds of existing machinery" [192, p. 5].

Thus, in the reminder of this chapter, I shall first start with a short description of some technical terms. Then, before we start with Turing's fascinating connectionist networks, classical Turing machines and some related machines shall briefly be presented.

2.1.1 Technical Terms

Turing started his discussion by a definition of some technical terms describing existent machinery:

Definition 2.1.1 (Discrete and continuous machinery)
We may call a machine "discrete" when it is natural to describe its possible states as a discrete set, the motion of a machine occurring by jumping from one state to another. The states of "continuous" machinery on the other hand form a continuous manifold and the behaviour of the machine is described by a curve on this manifold. All machinery can be regarded as continuous, but when it is possible to regard it as discrete it is usually best to do so. The states of discrete machinery will be described as "configurations" [192, p. 5]. ∎

Definition 2.1.2 (Controlling and active machinery)
Machinery may be described as "controlling" if it only deals with information. "Active" machinery is intended to produce some definite physical effect [192, p. 5]. ∎

These definitions are quite informal. Turing himself classified the brain as machinery with continuous controlling, but very similar to much discrete machinery [192, p. 5]. He clarified this classification later on with the following statement:

> "As we have mentioned, brains very nearly fall into this class (i.e., discrete controlling machinery), and there seems every reason to believe that they could have been made to fall genuinely into it without change in their essential properties. However, the property of being "discrete" is only an advantage for the theoretical investigator, and serves no evolutionary purpose, so we could not expect Nature to assist us by producing truly "discrete" brains" [192, p. 6].

Turing was convinced that the brain should be considered as a discrete state machine:

> "Turing's claim is that the only features of the brain relevant to thinking or intelligence are those which fall within the discrete-state-machine level of description" [90, p. 35].

On the other hand, he was aware that the nervous system on the physical level could not be considered as a discrete state machine [188]. Today, much discussion is still focused on that issue. "Can machines think?" [188]. A question that has no definite answer so far, and might never have one. Turing himself believed that machines can mimic any activity of the mind. Roger Penrose (and others) certainly do not share this point of view (see for example [141]). Further details will be discussed in Section 5.11. The rather philosophical *Mind* paper is a good introduction for the interested reader to Turing's machine-intelligence vision [188].

2.1.2 Turing Machines

Turing described in [185] (reprint in [46]) a certain type of machine called *logical computing machine (LCM)*. Today, this machine is more commonly known as the *Turing machine*. A Turing machine—an abstract computing device—is a finite-state machine associated with an external storage or memory medium (see Figure 2.1). For example, this storage medium can be a linear tape that is regarded as infinite in both directions. The machine is coupled to the tape through a head, which is situated, at each moment, on some square of the tape. The head then can read and write information from and to the tape. Furthermore, it can move to an adjacent square. A Turing machine computes via a sequence of discrete steps and its behaviour is always completely deterministic. The tape of a Turing machine is often considered as infinite in both (or one) direction. However, this view of idealization is physically completely unrealistic and only holds as an abstract model. A better approach is to view the tape as finite, but indefinitely extendible, i.e., whenever an additional square is needed, one can be attached to either end of the tape. The program of a Turing machine is normally given in the form of a discrete state transition diagram.

Many Turing machine variations have been proposed (e.g., multi-tape Turing machines, probabilistic Turing machines, multidimensional Turing machines, etc.), however, any variation can always be simulated (often with a loss of time) by a one-tape Turing machine.

For further reading about Turing machines, interested readers are referred to [46, 47, 59, 89, 125, 185].

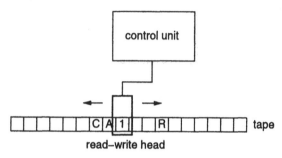

Fig. 2.1. Architecture of a Turing machine: finite state control unit, tape, and read-write head.

2.1.3 Universal Turing Machines

It is possible to program a Turing machine to accept the description of the program and input data of any other Turing machine computation, and to simulate that computation. Such a machine is called *universal logical computing machine* (ULCM) or *universal Turing machine* (UTM). The universal machine thus simply carries out the operations of the machine whose description was given on the tape. Today, one would rather say that the machines execute a *program*. The necessary components of the machine U are (1) a finite-state machine (the program of U) that controls the mobile head operating on the tape; (2) the data on the tape that describes the specialized Turing machine T to be simulated (the data of T, and (3) the program of T.

However, what is the interest of a UTM? Turing wrote:

> "The importance of the universal machine is clear. We do not need to have an infinity of different machines doing different jobs" [192, p. 7].

Figure 2.2 shows the organization of a UTM's tape as given in [125]. A first semi-infinite region contains the data of T's tape and a marker M indicating where T's head is currently located. The second region contains the current internal state Q and the current input symbol S of T. Finally, the third region is used to record the description of T, i.e., the three functions Q^+, S^+, and D^+ for each combination of Q and S. For an in-depth description of the UTM see [125, p. 132–144]

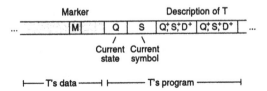

Fig. 2.2. The tape of a universal Turing machine U containing the description of a specialized machine T.

Finally, the most important thing to say about Turing machines is that—as an abstract model—they are functionally as powerful as any computer. This statement—misinterpreted many times—is generally known as the *Church-Turing thesis*. So far, the Church-Turing thesis has not been refuted. For more details about the thesis and hypercomputers—machines that compute beyond Turing machines—see also Section 5.11. For further reading, the interested reader is referred to Davis' new book about universal computers [47].

2.1.4 Practical Computing Machines

Turing was concerned with the enormous number of steps a Turing machine might need in order to complete a given task. He was conscious that this is mainly due to the way information is arranged on the tape. Often, the machine's head has to cover rather long distances between two operations and there was no real hope to compress data efficiently. He was further concerned about the finiteness of real machines but was aware that one can always find finite bounds to the number that are used. There is no way—at least so far—to deal with infinite precision on finite machines (see also Section 5.11) and thus, any real machine has to work with bounded numbers. From the construction of many real machines, Turing was naturally also aware that real machines store data in a different way and representation than Turing machines. The term *Practical Computing Machines* was introduced by Turing for real machines. In analogy with universal Turing machines, he also used the term *Universal Practical Computing Machines*. An answer to the question whether the real *Automatic Computing Machine (ACE)* machine[1] would be

---

[1] Many documents about the ACE are available online in the "Turing Archive for the History of Computing": http://www.alanturing.net.

truly universal if its memory capacity were infinite, was given in [192]. Turing concluded that "[...] there seems to be no way out of the difficulty but to introduce a tape" [192], a tape that might be extended *ad infinitum.*

In [192], further machines like *paper machines, partially random,* and *apparently partially random machines* are shortly described. We shall not discuss these machines here.

2.1.5 P-type Machines

A P-type unorganized machine [192] is not a neural network but a Turing machine without a tape. Initially, the machine description is, however, largely incomplete. For configurations that have missing actions, a random choice is made and the entry is tentatively added to the machine's description. The machine has two additional input lines: the *pleasure* (or *reward*) line and the *pain* (or *punishment*) line. Turing writes:

> "When a pain stimulus occurs, all tentative entries are cancelled, and when a pleasure stimulus occurs they are all made permanent" [192, p. 18].

This concept is certainly very interesting and is perhaps best compared with the reinforcement learning approach [174]. Turing studied P-type machines in the hope of discovering some *teaching policies* similar to the learning process of a child. Turing's experiments with P-type machines were not very successful. He writes:

> "The actual method by which the 'organizing' of the P-type machine was carried through is perhaps a little disappointing" [192, p. 20].

The problem was that the method he used to train the P-type's with external memory required considerable intelligence on the part of the trainer [39].

This type of machine is not further described in this book. The interested reader is referred to [39, 192].

2.2 Turing's Unorganized Machines

The term *unorganized machine* has been defined by Turing in a rather informal way. He introduced this kind of machine as a machine that is not designed for a precise purpose. Although the universal Turing machine—as its name suggests—is universal in the sense that it can perform any required task, the UTM cannot be re-configured and its architecture cannot be changed during operation. There is no doubt that Turing was inspired by the human nervous system when he conceived unorganized machines. The idea behind these machines (or rather networks) is that they are built up in a random manner and that they are trained (or organized) by means of an external agent (teacher). At the beginning, the machines are thus completely unorganized, comparable to an infants brain. "Then, by applying appropriate interference, mimicking education [...]" [192], the machine will be organized to produce a required behaviour.

It is important to note that Turing only proposed three types of unorganized machines in his 1948 paper [192]. Namely A-type, B-type, and P-type networks. He did not formally distinguish between B-type networks with interfering inputs and networks without interfering inputs. In this book, the distinction has been made: B-type nets without interfering inputs are still called B-type nets, on the other hand, B-type nets with interfering inputs are called BI-type nets (the "I" stands for interference). The term "BI-type nets" has been introduced by the author. All machines described in the present section have already been invented by Turing. Note that all other machines presented in that book have no basis in Turing's writings but are extensions of Turing's ideas.

2.2.1 Fundamentals and Definitions

Definition 2.2.1 (Turing unorganized machine (TUM))
A Turing unorganized machine (TUM) is a machine make up in a comparatively unsystematic and random way from some kind of standard components [192, p. 9]. ■

This definition matches well the basic concepts of connectionism (see also Section 1.3). Turing himself admitted that the same machine might be regarded by one man as organized and by another as unorganized [192, p. 9]. He gave an example of a typical unorganized machine:

Example 2.2.1 (Example of a typical unorganized machine)
"The machine is made up from a rather large number N of similar units. Each unit has two input terminals, and has an output terminal which can be connected to input terminals of (0 or more) other units. We may imagine that for each integer $r, 1 \leq r \leq N$, two numbers $i(r)$ and $j(r)$ are chosen at random from 1...N and that we connect the inputs of unit r to the outputs of units $i(r)$ and $j(r)$. All of the units are connected to a central synchronizing unit from which synchronizing pulses are emitted at more or less equal intervals of time. The times when these pulses arrive will be called "moments". Each unit is capable of having two states at each moment. These states may be called 0 and 1" [192, p. 9-10]. ■

An unorganized machine is thus updated synchronously, in discrete-time steps. The state of each unit is determined by the previous value of the two nodes connected as inputs. The transmission of information among neurons requires a unit time delay (one "moment"). Henceforth, *node, unit,* and *neuron* are synonymic, likewise *unorganized machine* and *artificial neural network.*

Definition 2.2.2 (State of a unit)
"The state is determined by the rule that the states of the units from which the input leads come are to be taken at the previous moment, multiplied together and the result subtracted from 1" [192, p. 10]   ∎

In a more formal way, the state of a unit can simply be defined as follows:

Corollary 2.2.3 (State of a unit)

$$state[t+1] \leftarrow 1 - x_1[t] \; x_2[t]$$
$$\leftarrow NOT(x_1[t] \; AND \; x_2[t])$$
$$\leftarrow \overline{x_1[t] \; AND \; x_2[t]}$$
$$\leftarrow x_1[t] \; NAND \; x_2[t] \qquad x_i \in \{0,1\}$$

(2.1)   ∎

The truth table of a *NAND* gate ("not AND") is quite simple and shown in Table 2.1.

x_1	x_2	output z
0	0	1
0	1	1
1	0	1
1	1	0

Table 2.1. Truth table of a NAND operator.

In terms of a digital system, the primitive unit that Turing describes can be straightforwardly defined as an *edge-triggered D flip-flop* with a preceding two-input NAND gate (Figure 2.3a). Figure 2.3b shows the functional table of a positive-edge-triggered *D* flip-flop: it samples its *D* input and changes its *Q* output only at the rising edge of the controlling clock (*CLK*) signal [206]. Figure 2.3c shows a symbolized network node with its two associated inputs x_1, x_2 and its output z as used by Turing. The central synchronizing unit that emits the pulses is the global clock generator of the digital system. Figure 2.4 shows the functional table of a primitive Turing unit (node).

Copeland and Proudfoot have defined a *propagation rule* and an *activation rule* [39, p. 364]. These two rules describe in a more abstract way the fact that each unit can be described as a D flip-flop with a preceding NAND gate.

Definition 2.2.4 (Propagation rule)
The net input into unit r at the moment t, net(r, t), is the product of the state i(r) at t − 1 and the state of j(r) at t − 1.   ∎

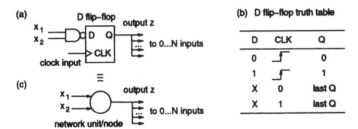

Fig. 2.3. A primitive Turing unit regarded as a digital system: (a) D flip-flop with a preceding two-input NAND gate; (b) Truth table of a positive-edge-triggered D flip-flop; (c) Symbolized network unit/node of an unorganized machine. Don't care values are marked with an X.

x_0	x_1	D	CLK	output z (Q)
0	0	1	⌐	1
1	0	1	⌐	1
1	0	1	⌐	1
1	1	0	⌐	0
X	X	X	0	last Q
X	X	X	1	last Q

Fig. 2.4. Functional table of a primitive Turing unit built up from a positive-edge-triggered D flip-flop with a preceding NAND gate. Don't care values are marked with an X.

Definition 2.2.5 (Activation rule)
 The state r at t is $1 - net(r,t)$. ∎

In modern terms, a Turing unorganized machine can be considered as a *random boolean network (RBN)*, also called *random binary recurrent network*. Modern neural networks are often organized in the form of several layers. Since unorganized machines are normally constructed at random, with no interconnection constraints, the layered structure does not really exist. Compared to a modern artificial neural network, e.g., a three-layer feed-forward network, an unorganized machine is thus probably more akin to the neural structure of the human brain. Turing even suggested that "[...] the cortex of the infant is an unorganized machine, which can be organized by suitable interfering training" [192, p. 16]. This statement might certainly be questioned since it largely oversimplifies the brain. The human cortex, especially the visual cortex, is just one of the most layered regions in the brain [220]. Another simple counter-argument is that there is no global clock in biological systems.

2.2.2 A-type Unorganized Machines

Turing defined an A-*type unorganized machine* as a machine built up from
units and connections as described in Example 2.2.1. This kind of machine
is the simplest unorganized machine and its architecture, once initialized,
cannot be modified. Figure 2.5 shows a very simple five unit A-type unorganized machine [192, p. 10]. From an initial internal machine state (machine
configuration), that machine state changes deterministically and will end up
in a fixed attractor or in a dynamic attractor with a fixed length (see also
Section 5.7). A possible machine state sequence of the machine from Figure
2.5 is shown in Table 2.2. It starts with the values indicated in the t-column.
Each time step ($t+1$, $t+2$, etc.), synchronized by the global clock generator,
changes the internal state of the machine.

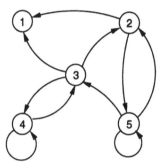

Fig. 2.5. Example of an A-type unorganized machine built up from five units. The
diagram only represents the architecture of the network and has nothing to do with
a state-machine diagram. Each node receives an input from exactly two nodes.

node	t	$t+1$	$t+2$	$t+3$	$t+4$	$t+5$	...
1	1	1	0	0	1	0	
2	1	1	1	0	1	0	
3	0	1	1	1	1	1	...
4	0	1	0	1	0	1	
5	1	0	1	0	1	0	

Table 2.2. Possible state sequence of the above five unit A-type unorganized machine.

2.2.3 B-type Unorganized Machines

Turing introduced a second type of machine, called B-type machine, "[...] not
because it is of any great intrinsic importance, but because it will be useful

later for illustrative purposes" [192]. However, his idea was clearly to open the possibility to reinforce successful and useful links and to cut useless ones. His deeper motivation was to build structures which allow for learning.

A B-type unorganized machine is an A-type machine where each connection in it has been replaced by a small A-type machine. The network shown in Figure 2.6 represents an abbreviation for a B-type link. Turing used a small square on the link to represent a B-type link. The nodes used within each replaced connection are called *primitive nodes*, the "main" network nodes are rather called *neurons*. Note, however, that neurons are primitive nodes too. This terminology is only used to distinguish the main nodes from the interconnection nodes.

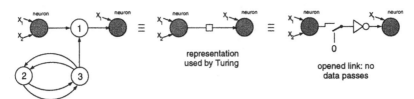

Fig. 2.6. Abbreviation for a B-type link. A B-type link is a small 3-node A-type machine that can be in three different internal states. The representation in the middle has been used by Turing. To the right, symbolic representation of the two states of operation (1) and (2).

It can be seen that, depending on its initial internal state, the A-type machine that forms the B-type link can be in three different conditions of operation [192, p. 11] (a very detailed analysis of the link shall be given in Section 2.3.2):

1. it may invert the incoming signal (*closed* or *enabled* connection),
2. it may interrupt the incoming signal and put a constant 1 on its output (*opened* or *disabled* connection), or
3. it may act as in (1) and (2) in alternation.

A link is considered as *closed* or *enabled* when it passes the signal from one node to another. On the other hand, a link is considered as *opened* or *disabled* when no signal passes. During operation, the internal state of the link cannot be changed. Compared to an A-type unorganized machine, a B-type machine can have not only closed but both, opened and closed links. The states of operation of a B-type link suggest that it might be considered as a sort of *fixed switch* (Copeland and Proudfoot rather talked about an *elementary memory* [39, p. 365]). Due to node (1) (see Figure 2.6) in each link, signals passed through it get an additional delay of one clock cycle. In the next few sections, we shall see how this kind of link is used to modify, by means of an external teacher, the internal state of the link.

Figure 2.7 shows a simple five unit B-type unorganized machine. This machine has been constructed on the basis of the A-type machine from Figure 2.5: each direct link of the A-type machine has been replaced by a B-type link as shown in Figure 2.6. It directly follows that each B-type machine can be considered as an A-type machine. The inverse is not valid since it is very unlikely that one gets a B-type machine when randomly constructing an A-type unorganized machine.

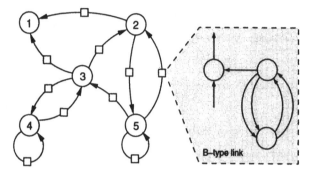

Fig. 2.7. Example of a B-type unorganized machine built up from five units.

2.2.4 Turing's "Education" of Machinery

The unorganized machines described so far did not allow any interference from the outside world. Once initialized, the machine works in a deterministic manner that only depends on the initial configuration. It would clearly be interesting to modify the configuration and the architecture of a given machine during operation and to adapt it to a certain task. Turing talks about a "[...] machine as being *modifiable*" when it is possible to "[...] alter the behaviour of a machine very radically [...]" [192]. He distinguished two kinds of interference with machinery:

1. *screwdriver interference*,
2. *paper interference*.

Screwdriver interference is the extreme form in which parts of the machine are removed and replaced by others. Paper interference consists in the mere communication of information to the machine, which alters its behaviour. Turing also spoke about machines that modify themselves and he classified the operations of a machine into two classes:

1. *normal operations*,
2. *self-modifying operations*.

We regard a machine as *unaltered* when only normal operations are performed. An operation is self-modifying when the internal storage of the machine (i.e., the tape of a machine) is altered.

"It would be quite unfair to expect a machine straight from the factory to compete on equal terms with a university graduate" [192]. Turing's vision of machine education is probably best summarized by the following statement:

> "If we are trying to produce an intelligent machine, and are following the human model as closely as we can, we should begin with a machine with very little capacity to carry out elaborate operations or to react in a disciplined manner to orders (taking the form of interference). Then by applying appropriate interference, mimicking education, we should hope to modify the machine until it could be relied on to produce definite reactions to certain commands" [192, p. 14].

However, what exactly is meant by "appropriate interference"? Turing wrote further:

> "[...] that with suitable initial conditions they [e.g., unorganized machines] will do any required job, given sufficient time and provided the number of units is sufficient. In particular with a B-type unorganized machine with sufficient units one can find initial conditions which will make it into a universal machine with a given storage capacity" [192, p. 15].

Unfortunately, Turing did not give formal proof of this hypothesis because "[...] it lies rather too far outside the main argument". As we shall see in Section 2.3.6, not all unorganized networks might be used to build universal machines. Section 5.2 will provide further details about the computational power of unorganized machines.

"Appropriate interference", however, remained a vague expression in Turing's papers and he never really went into details. One of his most concrete unorganized-machine organizing experiments was probably the P-type machine (see Section 2.1.5), also called *pleasure-pain system* [192]. In the next section we shall see how a simple B-type network, that, once initialized, is no longer modifiable, could be transformed into a machine modifiable, i.e., "trainable" by an external supervisor. So far, the supervisor is not further detailed, but we shall see in Section 4 different means of organizing unorganized machines. It is interesting that Turing himself already mentioned "genetical" or "evolutionary" search in his 1948 paper—a optimization method that will be further explored in this book.

2.2.5 BI-type Unorganized Machines

With a simple A-type or B-type machine, the possibility of interference which could set it into an appropriate initial configuration has not been arranged for. "However, it is not difficult to think of appropriate methods by which this could be done" [192, p. 15]. Figure 2.8 shows a possible solution: two additional inputs I_A and I_B have been added to a normal B-type link as previously presented in Figure 2.6. Hopefully, it is now clear why Turing first introduced the B-type link seen in Section 2.2.3. From the beginning, his goal was to construct a sort of switch from all and the same primitive elements, i.e., nodes or neurons. Copeland and Proudfoot used the term *introverted pair* [39] for the pair of nodes within a B-type node. At a first glance, a B-type link might seem rather complicated for a simple switch, however, it is the simplest possible solution that can be realized by means of the type of node he used.

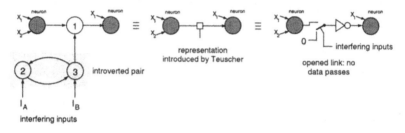

Fig. 2.8. BI-type link: B-type link with interfering inputs I_A and I_B that affect the internal state of the interconnection switch.

A BI-type machine (the "I" stands for interference) is defined as a machine where each network connection consists of a link as shown in Figure 2.8. By supplying appropriate signals to the *interfering inputs* I_A, I_B—Turing called these signals simply A and B and he used no special name for a B-type machine with interfering inputs—we can get the connection into condition (1) or (2) as explained in Section 2.2.3. By means of this type of link, an external or internal agent can organize an initially random B-type machine by disabling and enabling connections within it: successful and useful links are reinforced, useless ones are cut. Turing wrote: "The process of setting up these initial conditions so that the machine will carry out some particular useful task may be called 'organizing the machine'. 'Organizing' is thus a form of 'modification'" [192, p. 16]. Organizing a machine might, however, not only be a question of setting up *initial conditions*. It would clearly be interesting to change the link's state *online*, during operation.

2.3 Formalization and Analysis of Unorganized Machines

So far, we have seen an overview on A-type, B-type, and BI-type unorganized machines. The goal of this section is to provide one of several possible mathematical formalizations of Turing's connectionist machines. This should make for a better understanding of their characteristics and intrinsic dynamics.

Let N be the total number of nodes in the network (including input and output nodes), I the number of input nodes, O the number of output nodes, and D the number of computing nodes:

Definition 2.3.1 (Neuron sets)

$$\mathcal{N} = set\ of\ network\ nodes, \quad |\mathcal{N}| = N \tag{2.2}$$

$$\mathcal{I} \in \mathcal{N} = set\ of\ input\ nodes, \quad |\mathcal{I}| = I \tag{2.3}$$

$$\mathcal{D} \in \mathcal{N} = set\ of\ computing\ nodes, \quad |\mathcal{D}| = D \tag{2.4}$$

$$\mathcal{O} \in \mathcal{D} = set\ of\ output\ nodes, \quad |\mathcal{O}| = O \tag{2.5}$$

■

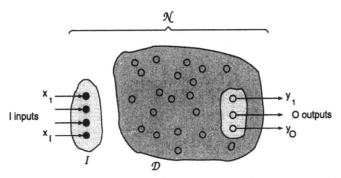

Fig. 2.9. Architecture of a generic unorganized machine with input and output nodes. Turing only described unorganized machines without inputs and outputs.

Figure 2.9 shows a generic unorganized machine with input and output nodes. Turing only described unorganized machines without inputs nor outputs. One can easily verify the following relations:

Definition 2.3.2 (Neuron set relations)

$$\mathcal{N} = \mathcal{I} \cup \mathcal{D} \tag{2.6}$$

$$\mathcal{D} = \mathcal{N} \backslash \mathcal{I} \tag{2.7}$$

$$N = I + D \tag{2.8}$$

■

According to Definition 2.2.2 and Corollary 2.2.3, the neuron transfer function that is valid for any node in Turing's unorganized machines can be re-written in a slightly different way:

Definition 2.3.3 (Turing neuron transfer function: NAND)

$$z = f(x, y) = 1 - xy \qquad x, y \in \{0, 1\} \tag{2.9}$$

■

In the following, the different kind of unorganized machines seen so far will be formalized.

2.3.1 Formalization of A-type Networks

An A-type machine with inputs and outputs can be defined in a formal way as follows (this definition is inspired by the definition of a neural network given in [150]):

Definition 2.3.4 (A-type unorganized machine)
An A-type unorganized machine is a tuple $\mathcal{M} = (\mathcal{I}, \mathcal{N}, \mathcal{O}, \mathcal{E})$ consisting of a set of $\mathcal{I} \in \mathcal{N}$ of input sites, a set $\mathcal{N} \backslash \mathcal{I}$ of computing units, a set $\mathcal{O} \in \mathcal{N} \backslash \mathcal{I}$ of output sites, and a set $\mathcal{E}$ of directed edges. A directed edge is a tuple (u, v) whereby $u \in \mathcal{N}$ and $v \in \mathcal{N} \backslash \mathcal{I}$. An input site $r \in \mathcal{I}$ has the value $x_r \in \{0, 1\}$ at the moment t, where $x_r[t]$ is the input value of x_r at the moment $t - 1$. The net input into unit $r \in \mathcal{N} \backslash \mathcal{I}$ at the moment t, $net(r, t)$, is the product of the state $i(r) \in \mathcal{N} \backslash \mathcal{I}$ at $t - 1$ and the state of $j(r) \in \mathcal{N} \backslash \mathcal{I}$ at $t - 1$. The state $r \in \mathcal{N} \backslash \mathcal{I}$ at t is $1 - net(r, t)$. ■

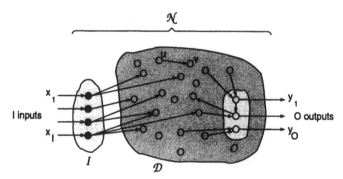

Fig. 2.10. Structure of an A-type unorganized machine with inputs and outputs.

Figure 2.10 shows the structure of an A-type unorganized machine with associated inputs and outputs. As already seen in Section 2.2.1, Figure 2.3, an A-type node can be defined as follows:

Definition 2.3.5 (A-type node)
An A-type node consists of a D flip-flop with a preceding two-input NAND gate (see Figure 2.3). ∎

As for an input node, it simply consists of a single input D flip-flop without a preceding NAND gate that samples the input signal x_i at each positive clock edge. Input units have mainly been added to provide a non-inverted synchronized signal with an internal machine clock.

Definition 2.3.6 (Input site)
An A-type input site consists of a D flip-flop. ∎

Definition 2.3.7 (A-type neuron output)
The output $d_n[t + 1]$ of a unit n at time $t + 1$ depends on the previous outputs of the units $d_i[t], i \in 1, ..., N$ and $d_j[t], j \in 1, ..., N$ connected as inputs to unit d_n (see Figure 2.11(a)). The output value of a single node n is given by Equation 2.10:

$$d_n[t + 1] = \begin{cases} x_n[t] & \text{if } n \in \mathcal{I} \\ f(d_i[t], d_j[t]) & \text{if } n \in \mathcal{D}, \ i = 1, ..., N, \ j = 1, ..., N \end{cases}$$

$$= \begin{cases} x_n[t] & \text{if } n \in \mathcal{I} \\ 1 - d_i[t] \, d_j[t] & \text{if } n \in \mathcal{D}, \ i = 1, ..., N, \ j = 1, ..., N \end{cases}$$

$$(2.10)$$

∎

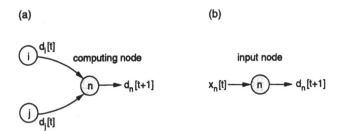

(a)   (b)

computing node   input node

Fig. 2.11. Definition of the output $d_n[t + 1]$ of an A-type neuron n. The output of a computing node (a) depends on its two inputs whereas the output of an input node only depends on its direct input (b).

Each one of the computing nodes $\mathcal{D}$ can be considered as an output node:

Definition 2.3.8 (A-type network output)

$$y_n[t + 1] = d_n[t + 1] \qquad n \in \mathcal{O} \tag{2.11}$$

∎

The architecture of a given network is described by means of a connection matrix. A "1" set at position c_{ij} of the connection matrix C indicates a connection from node $i \in \mathcal{N}$ to node $j \in \mathcal{D}$. If two parallel connections exist from $i \in \mathcal{N}$ to node $j \in \mathcal{D}$, then a "2" is set at position c_{ij} (see Definition 2.3.9).

Definition 2.3.9 (Network connection matrix)

$$c_{ij} = \begin{cases} 1 & \text{if link from } i \text{ to } j, \\ 2 & \text{if double link from } i \text{ to } j, \\ 0 & \text{otherwise.} \end{cases} \tag{2.12}$$

$$C_{N \times N} = \begin{bmatrix} 0 \ldots 0 \ c_{1(I+1)} & \cdots & c_{1N} \\ \vdots & \vdots & \vdots & \vdots \\ 0 \ldots 0 \ c_{N(I+1)} & \cdots & c_{NN} \end{bmatrix} \tag{2.13}$$

∎

The elements c_{ij}, $i = 1, ..., N$, $j = 1, ..., I$ are set to 0 since no connection can end on an input node. As each neuron receives exactly two inputs, the following property holds for C:

Corollary 2.3.10 (Connection matrix structure)

$$\forall \ \text{column } j = I + 1, ..., N : \sum_{i=0}^{N} c_{ij} = 2 \tag{2.14}$$

∎

In other words, the sum of each column $j = I + 1, ..., N$ of the matrix C is equal to 2.

The dynamics of an A-type network can now be formalized in vectorized form:

Definition 2.3.11 (A-type network dynamics)

$$\vec{d_N}[t] = \begin{bmatrix} d_1[t] \\ \vdots \\ d_I[t] \\ d_{I+1}[t] \\ \vdots \\ d_{N-O+1}[t] \\ \vdots \\ d_N[t] \end{bmatrix} \qquad \text{(current network state)} \tag{2.15}$$

$$\overrightarrow{x_N^+}[t] = \begin{bmatrix} 1 - x_1[t] \\ \vdots \\ 1 - x_I[t] \\ 0 \\ \vdots \\ 0 \end{bmatrix} \qquad (expanded\ input\ vector) \qquad (2.16)$$

$$\overrightarrow{d_N}[t+1] = \overrightarrow{\phi}\,(C^T \overrightarrow{d_N}[t]) - \overrightarrow{x_N^+}[t] \qquad (network\ state) \qquad (2.17)$$

$$\overrightarrow{y_O}[t+1] = \overrightarrow{d}_O[t+1] \qquad (network\ output)$$

$$= \begin{bmatrix} d_{N-O+1}[t+1] \\ \vdots \\ d_N[t+1] \end{bmatrix} \qquad (vector\ with\ nodes \in \mathcal{O}) \qquad (2.18) \qquad \blacksquare$$

Definition 2.3.12 shows a vectorized form of the scalar neuron transfer function (see Definition 2.3.3). The vector $d_N[t]$ contains the values of *all* nodes in the network.

Definition 2.3.12 (Matrix form NAND transfer function)

$$\phi(x) = \begin{cases} 0 & if\ x = 2, \\ 1 & otherwise. \end{cases} \qquad (2.19)$$

$$\overrightarrow{\phi}\,(x) = \begin{bmatrix} \phi(x) \\ \vdots \\ \phi(x) \end{bmatrix} \qquad (2.20) \qquad \blacksquare$$

The above definitions are best illustrated with a simple example:

Example 2.3.1 (A-type network dynamics)
Consider the A-type network as described in Figure 2.12 where $|\mathcal{I}| = I = 2$, $|\mathcal{O}| = O = 2$, $|\mathcal{N}| = N = 7$. The numbers in italics indicate the initial state at time $t = 0$.

The connection matrix C of the above network shown in Figure 2.12 is as follows:

$$C_{7\times7} = \begin{bmatrix} 0 & 0 & 1 & 0 & 0 & 0 & 0 \\ 0 & 0 & 1 & 0 & 1 & 0 & 0 \\ 0 & 0 & 0 & 0 & 0 & 1 & 0 \\ 0 & 0 & 0 & 1 & 0 & 0 & 1 \\ 0 & 0 & 0 & 1 & 0 & 1 & 0 \\ 0 & 0 & 0 & 0 & 0 & 0 & 1 \\ 0 & 0 & 0 & 0 & 1 & 0 & 0 \end{bmatrix}$$

Figure 2.12 directly leads us to the initial network state-vector $\vec{d_7}[t]$ (values in italics) and to the expanded input vector $\vec{x_7^+}[t]$.

$$\vec{d_7}[t] = \begin{bmatrix} 1 \\ 0 \\ 0 \\ 1 \\ 1 \\ 1 \\ 0 \end{bmatrix}$$

$$\vec{x_7^+}[t] = \begin{bmatrix} 1 - x_1[t] \\ 1 - x_2[t] \\ 0 \\ 0 \\ 0 \\ 0 \\ 0 \end{bmatrix} = \begin{bmatrix} 1 \\ 0 \\ 0 \\ 0 \\ 0 \\ 0 \\ 0 \end{bmatrix}$$

Next, the state $\vec{d}[t+1]$ at time $t+1$ is calculated by Equation 2.17:

$$\vec{d_7}[t+1] = \vec{\phi}(C_{7\times 7}^T \vec{d_7}[t]) - \vec{x_7^+}[t]$$

$$= \vec{\phi}\left(\begin{bmatrix} 0 & 0 & 0 & 0 & 0 & 0 & 0 \\ 0 & 0 & 0 & 0 & 0 & 0 & 0 \\ 1 & 1 & 0 & 0 & 0 & 0 & 0 \\ 0 & 0 & 0 & 1 & 1 & 0 & 0 \\ 0 & 1 & 0 & 0 & 0 & 0 & 1 \\ 0 & 0 & 1 & 0 & 1 & 0 & 0 \\ 0 & 0 & 0 & 1 & 0 & 1 & 0 \end{bmatrix} \begin{bmatrix} 1 \\ 0 \\ 0 \\ 1 \\ 1 \\ 1 \\ 0 \end{bmatrix} \right) - \begin{bmatrix} 1 \\ 0 \\ 0 \\ 0 \\ 0 \\ 0 \\ 0 \end{bmatrix} = \vec{\phi}\left(\begin{bmatrix} 0 \\ 0 \\ 1 \\ 1 \\ 0 \\ 1 \\ 2 \end{bmatrix} \right) - \begin{bmatrix} 1 \\ 0 \\ 0 \\ 0 \\ 0 \\ 0 \\ 0 \end{bmatrix}$$

$$= \begin{bmatrix} 1 \\ 1 \\ 1 \\ 1 \\ 1 \\ 1 \\ 0 \end{bmatrix} - \begin{bmatrix} 1 \\ 0 \\ 0 \\ 0 \\ 0 \\ 0 \\ 0 \end{bmatrix} = \begin{bmatrix} 0 \\ 1 \\ 1 \\ 1 \\ 1 \\ 1 \\ 0 \end{bmatrix}$$

And last but not least, the network output is calculated by Equation 2.18.

$$\vec{y_2}[t+1] = \begin{bmatrix} d_{N-O+1}[t+1] \\ \vdots \\ d_N[t+1] \end{bmatrix} = \begin{bmatrix} d_{7-2+1}[t+1] \\ \vdots \\ d_7[t+1] \end{bmatrix} = \begin{bmatrix} d_6[t+1] \\ d_7[t+1] \end{bmatrix} = \begin{bmatrix} 1 \\ 0 \end{bmatrix}$$

■

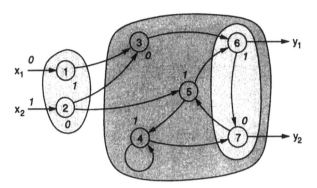

Fig. 2.12. Example: A simple A-type network with two inputs, five network nodes, and two outputs. The values in italics indicate the initial state at time $t = 0$.

2.3.2 Formalization of B-type Links

Before we formalize and analyze the dynamics of a B-type network, we must first take a look at the B-type link. As already presented in Section 2.2.3, a B-type link is a small 3-node A-type network with one input and one output, both connected to the same neuron. A B-type link can be regarded as a sequential digital system [206] as depicted in Figure 2.13.

	Q_2	Q_3	Q_2^+	Q_3^+	connection	state	condition
S_0	0	0	1	1	enabled/closed	meta stable	(3)
S_1	0	1	0	1	enabled/closed	stable	(1)
S_2	1	0	1	0	disabled/opened	stable	(2)
S_3	1	1	0	0	disabled/opened	meta stable	(3)

Table 2.3. Possible states of a B-type link. Q_2 and Q_3 represent the current state of the sequential digital system whereas Q_2^+ and Q_3^+ is the future state, assigned after one clock step.

Table 2.3 summarizes the possible internal states of a B-type link (see also Section 2.2.3). The different conditions of operation are probably better recognized if the link is reduced to elemental logical functions as shown in Figure 2.14. When the link is in state S_1, the signal is inverted and traverses the link with a delay of one clock cycle (enabled/closed link). In state S_2, no signal passes and the link's output is always set to 1 (disabled/opened link).

As the input x_1 of the link is directly connected to the same node as the output y_1, this small A-type machine is somewhat unusual and the connection matrix does not match with Corollary 2.14. The following equations hold (2.21-2.25):

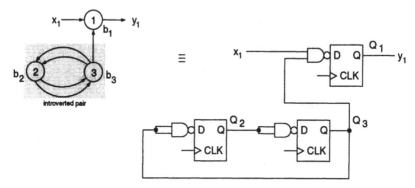

Fig. 2.13. A B-type link regarded as a sequential digital system.

$$B = \begin{bmatrix} 0 & 0 & 0 \\ 0 & 0 & 2 \\ 1 & 2 & 0 \end{bmatrix} \qquad \text{(B-type link connection matrix)} \qquad (2.21)$$

$$\overrightarrow{b}[t] = \begin{bmatrix} b_1[t] \\ b_2[t] \\ b_3[t] \end{bmatrix} \qquad \text{(B-type link state vector)} \qquad (2.22)$$

$$\overrightarrow{x^+}[t] = \begin{bmatrix} x_1[t] \\ 0 \\ 0 \end{bmatrix} \qquad \text{(expanded B-type input vector)} \qquad (2.23)$$

$$\overrightarrow{b}[t+1] = \overrightarrow{\phi}(B^T \overrightarrow{b}[t] + \overrightarrow{x^+}[t]) \qquad \text{(link state)} \qquad (2.24)$$

$$y_1[t+1] = b_1[t+1] \qquad \text{(link output)} \qquad (2.25)$$

Copeland and Proudfoot refer to the state of a B-type link as the "determining condition" [39]. The small A-type machine incorporated in the B-type link is a sequential system that functions as a memory: the state of the link only depends on the values of node 2 (Q_2) and node 3 (Q_3). Copeland and Proudfoot wrote: "Thus an introverted pair functions as an elementary memory" [39].

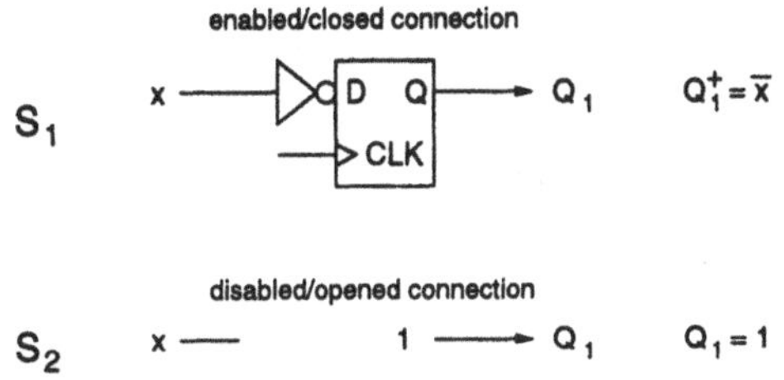

enabled/closed connection

S_1 x $\longrightarrow$ [D Q | CLK] $\longrightarrow$ Q_1 $Q_1^+ = \bar{x}$

disabled/opened connection

S_2 x $\longrightarrow$ 1 $\longrightarrow$ Q_1 $Q_1 = 1$

Fig. 2.14. A B-type link can be reduced to a simpler, but functionally equivalent unit. The state of the unit only depends on the initial values of Q_2 and Q_3.

Example 2.3.2 (B-type link dynamics)

Suppose that a given B-type link has the value 0 on its input and that the initial state vector is given by:

$$\overrightarrow{b}[t] = \begin{bmatrix} b_1[t] \\ b_2[t] \\ b_3[t] \end{bmatrix} = \begin{bmatrix} 0 \\ 0 \\ 1 \end{bmatrix}$$

According to Table 2.3, the link is in condition (2) and thus functions like an inverter (connection enabled/opened).

$$\overrightarrow{x^+}[t] = \begin{bmatrix} x_1[t] \\ 0 \\ 0 \end{bmatrix} = \begin{bmatrix} 0 \\ 0 \\ 0 \end{bmatrix}$$

$$\overrightarrow{b}[t+1] = \overrightarrow{\phi}(B^T \overrightarrow{b}[t] + \overrightarrow{x^+}[t]) = \begin{bmatrix} 0 & 0 & 1 \\ 0 & 0 & 2 \\ 0 & 2 & 0 \end{bmatrix} \begin{bmatrix} 0 \\ 0 \\ 1 \end{bmatrix} + \begin{bmatrix} 0 \\ 0 \\ 0 \end{bmatrix}$$

$$= \overrightarrow{\phi}(\begin{bmatrix} 1 \\ 2 \\ 0 \end{bmatrix} + \begin{bmatrix} 0 \\ 0 \\ 0 \end{bmatrix}) = \begin{bmatrix} 1 \\ 0 \\ 1 \end{bmatrix}$$

The above result shows that the state of the node ($b_2[t] = b_2[t+1]$, $b_3[t] = b_3[t+1]$) remains unchanged. The link output is 1:

$$y_1[t+1] = b_1[t+1] = 1$$

The same calculus can be done using different initial conditions. Let's demonstrate that the link is meta stable if in condition (3) (see Table 2.3). However, this time we set the input x_1 to 1.

$$\vec{b}\,[t] = \begin{bmatrix} 0 \\ 1 \\ 1 \end{bmatrix}$$

$$\vec{x}^+[t] = \begin{bmatrix} x_1[t] \\ 0 \\ 0 \end{bmatrix} = \begin{bmatrix} 1 \\ 0 \\ 0 \end{bmatrix}$$

At time $t+1$, the state is:

$$\vec{b}\,[t+1] = \vec{\phi}\,(\begin{bmatrix} 0\,0\,1 \\ 0\,0\,2 \\ 0\,2\,0 \end{bmatrix} \begin{bmatrix} 0 \\ 1 \\ 1 \end{bmatrix} + \begin{bmatrix} 1 \\ 0 \\ 0 \end{bmatrix})$$

$$= \vec{\phi}\,(\begin{bmatrix} 1 \\ 2 \\ 2 \end{bmatrix} + \begin{bmatrix} 1 \\ 0 \\ 0 \end{bmatrix}) = \begin{bmatrix} 0 \\ 0 \\ 0 \end{bmatrix}$$

$$y_1[t+1] = b_1[t+1] = 0$$

Then, at time $t+2$, the state is:

$$\vec{b}\,[t+2] = \vec{\phi}\,(\begin{bmatrix} 0\,0\,1 \\ 0\,0\,2 \\ 0\,2\,0 \end{bmatrix} \begin{bmatrix} 1 \\ 0 \\ 0 \end{bmatrix} + \begin{bmatrix} 1 \\ 0 \\ 0 \end{bmatrix})$$

$$= \vec{\phi}\,(\begin{bmatrix} 0 \\ 0 \\ 0 \end{bmatrix} + \begin{bmatrix} 1 \\ 0 \\ 0 \end{bmatrix}) = \begin{bmatrix} 1 \\ 1 \\ 1 \end{bmatrix}$$

$$y_1[t+2] = b_1[t+2] = 1$$

And the last step shows, that the state at time $t+3$ is equivalent to the state at time $t+1$:

$$\vec{b}\,[t+3] = \vec{\phi}\,(\begin{bmatrix} 0\,0\,1 \\ 0\,0\,2 \\ 0\,2\,0 \end{bmatrix} \begin{bmatrix} 1 \\ 1 \\ 1 \end{bmatrix} + \begin{bmatrix} 1 \\ 0 \\ 0 \end{bmatrix})$$

$$= \vec{\phi}\,(\begin{bmatrix} 1 \\ 2 \\ 2 \end{bmatrix} + \begin{bmatrix} 1 \\ 0 \\ 0 \end{bmatrix}) = \begin{bmatrix} 0 \\ 0 \\ 0 \end{bmatrix}$$

$$y_1[t+3] = b_1[t+3] = 0$$

■

2.3.3 Formalization of B-type Networks

A B-type machine with inputs and outputs can be defined in a formal way as follows (this definition is inspired by the definition of a neural network given in [150]):

Definition 2.3.13 (B-type unorganized machine)
A B-type unorganized machine (Figure 2.15) is a tuple $\mathcal{M} = (\mathcal{I}, \mathcal{N}, \mathcal{O}, \mathcal{L})$ consisting of a set of $I \in \mathcal{N}$ input sites, a set $\mathcal{N}\backslash\mathcal{I}$ of computing units, a set $\mathcal{O} \in \mathcal{N}\backslash\mathcal{I}$ of output sites, and a set $\mathcal{L}$ of links. A link is a tuple (M, u, v) whereby M is a 3-node A-type machine according to Figure 2.6, $u \in \mathcal{N}$ and $v \in \mathcal{N}\backslash\mathcal{I}$. An input site $r \in \mathcal{I}$ has the value $x_r \in \{0,1\}$ at the moment t, where $x_r[t]$ is the input value of x_r at the moment $t-1$. The net input into unit $r \in \mathcal{N}\backslash\mathcal{I}$ at the moment t, $net(r,t)$, is the product of the state $i(r) \in \mathcal{N}\backslash\mathcal{I}$ at $t-1$ and the state of $j(r) \in \mathcal{N}\backslash\mathcal{I}$ at $t-1$. The state $r \in \mathcal{N}\backslash\mathcal{I}$ at t is $1 - net(r,t)$ ∎

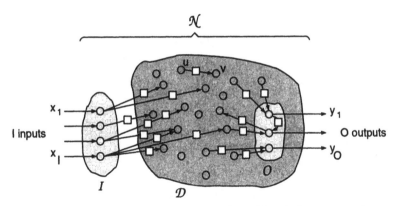

Fig. 2.15. Structure of a B-type unorganized machine with inputs and outputs. Each link can be considered as a sort of static switch that is either enabled (the signal passes) or disabled (the signal is interrupted and a 1 is on the link's output).

Definition 2.3.14 (B-type neuron output)
Figure 2.16(a) shows that the output $d_n[t+1]$ of a unit n at time $t+1$ depends on the previous outputs of the units $d_i[t], i \in 1, ..., N$, $d_j[t], j \in 1, ..., N$ connected as inputs to unit d_n, and on the internal state of the B-type links. $l_{in}[t]$ and $l_{jn}[t]$ are calculated by Equation 2.25. ∎

(a)   (b)

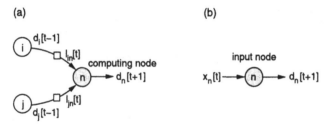

Fig. 2.16. Definition of the output $d_n[t+1]$ of a B-type neuron n. The output of a computing node (a) depends on its two inputs $l_{in}[t]$ and $l_{jn}[t]$ whereas the output of an input node only depends on its direct input $x_n[t]$ (b).

$$d_n[t+1] = \begin{cases} x_n[t] & \text{if } n \in \mathcal{I} \\ f(l_{in}[t], l_{jn}[t]) & \text{if } n \in \mathcal{D}, \; i = 1, ..., N, \; j = 1, ..., N \end{cases}$$

$$= \begin{cases} x_n[t] & \text{if } n \in \mathcal{I} \\ 1 - l_{in}[t] \, l_{jn}[t] & \text{if } n \in \mathcal{D}, \; i = 1, ..., N, \; j = 1, ..., N \end{cases}$$

(2.26)

2.3.4 Formalization of BI-type Links

Figure 2.17 shows the representation of a BI-type link in the form of a sequential digital system. A BI-type link is best analyzed by means of a state machine where x, I_A, and I_B are inputs and $y = Q_1$ an output. Starting from the digital system of Figure 2.17, a state table [206] is drawn (Table 2.4). Each line represents a state of the system, each column an input configuration. The entries in the table are the output y and the future state of the machine $(Q_1^+ Q_2^+ Q_3^+)$.

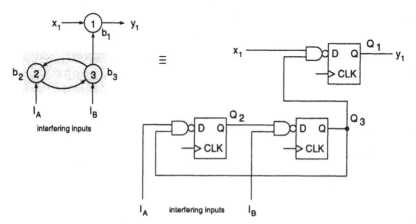

Fig. 2.17. A BI-type link regarded as a sequential digital system. The interfering inputs I_A and I_B are used to change the internal state of the link.

$x, I_A I_B$							
0,00	0,01	0,10	0,11	1,00	1,01	1,10	1,11
a=000 1,111	1,111	1,111	1,111	1,111	1,111	1,111	1,111
b=001 1,111	1,111	1,101	1,101	0,011	0,011	0,001	0,001
c=010 1,111	1,110	1,111	1,110	1,111	1,110	1,111	1,110
d=011 1,111	1,110	1,101	1,100	0,011	0,010	0,001	0,000
e=100 1,111	1,111	1,111	1,111	1,111	1,111	1,111	1,111
f=101 1,111	1,111	1,101	1,101	0,011	0,011	0,001	0,001
g=110 1,111	1,110	1,111	1,110	1,111	1,110	1,111	1,110
h=111 1,111	1,110	1,101	1,100	0,011	0,010	0,001	0,000
$Q_1 Q_2 Q_3$ $y = Q_1^+, Q_1^+ Q_2^+ Q_3^+$							

Table 2.4. State table of a BI-type link with interfering inputs I_A and I_B. Note that $Q_1^+ = y$.

The state table from Table 2.4 can be simplified since there are different states that have equal lines. The simplified state table is shown in Table 2.5.

$x, I_A I_B$							
0,00	0,01	0,10	0,11	1,00	1,01	1,10	1,11
a, e 1,h	1,h	1,h	1,h	1,h	1,h	1,h	1,h
b, f 1,h	1,h	1,f	1,f	0,d	0,d	0,b	0,b
c, g 1,h	1,g	1,h	1,g	1,h	1,g	1,h	1,g
d, h 1,h	1,g	1,f	1,e	0,d	0,c	0,b	0,a
current state $y = Q_1^+$, next state							

Table 2.5. Simplification of the BI-type link state table.

Then, a final state assignment is made (see Table 2.6) and the resulting minimal state machine can be easily drawn (see Figure 2.18).

$x, I_A I_B$							
0,00	0,01	0,10	0,11	1,00	1,01	1,10	1,11
$S_0 = 00$ $1, S_3$	$1, S_3$	$1, S_3$	$1, S_3$	$1, S_3$	$1, S_3$	$1, S_3$	$1, S_3$
$S_1 = 01$ $1, S_3$	$1, S_3$	$1, S_1$	$1, S_1$	$0, S_3$	$0, S_3$	$0, S_1$	$0, S_1$
$S_2 = 10$ $1, S_3$	$1, S_2$	$1, S_3$	$1, S_2$	$1, S_3$	$1, S_2$	$1, S_3$	$1, S_2$
$S_3 = 11$ $1, S_3$	$1, S_2$	$1, S_1$	$1, S_0$	$0, S_3$	$0, S_2$	$0, S_1$	$0, S_0$
current state $y = Q_1^+$, next state							
$= Q_2 Q_3$							

Table 2.6. Final state assignment where $S_0 = \{a, e\}, S_1 = \{b, f\}, S_2 = \{c, g\}, S_3 = \{d, h\}$. Note that Q_1 has no relevance for the state machine evolution and therefore has been deleted.

The connection matrix of a BI-type link is slightly different from a B-type link connection matrix (see Equation 2.21) because of the two interfering inputs. The following equations formalize the dynamics of the BI-type network (2.27-2.31):

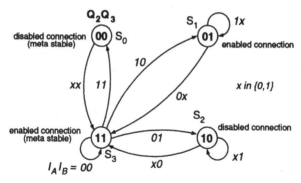

Fig. 2.18. State diagram of a BI-type link according to the final state Table 2.6. The state of the link can be changed by applying appropriate signals to I_A and I_B.

$$BI = \begin{bmatrix} 0\ 0\ 0 \\ 0\ 0\ 1 \\ 1\ 1\ 0 \end{bmatrix} \qquad \text{(BI-type connection matrix)} \qquad (2.27)$$

$$\overrightarrow{bi}[t] = \begin{bmatrix} b_1[t] \\ b_2[t] \\ b_3[t] \end{bmatrix} \qquad \text{(BI-type link state vector)} \qquad (2.28)$$

$$\overrightarrow{x^+}[t] = \begin{bmatrix} 1 - x_1[t] \\ 1 - I_A[t-1] \\ 1 - I_B[t-1] \end{bmatrix} \qquad \text{(BI-type input vector)} \qquad (2.29)$$

$$\overrightarrow{bi}[t+1] = \overrightarrow{\phi}\,(BI^T\,\overrightarrow{bi}[t]) - \overrightarrow{x^+}[t] \qquad (2.30)$$

$$y_1[t+1] = bi_1[t+1] \qquad \text{(link output)} \qquad (2.31)$$

2.3.5 Formalization of BI-type Networks

Similar to a B-type machine, a BI-type machine with inputs and outputs might be defined in a formal way as follows (this definition is inspired by the definition of a neural network given in [150]):

Definition 2.3.15 (BI-type unorganized machine)
 A BI-type unorganized machine (Figure 2.19) is a tuple $\mathcal{M} = (\mathcal{I}, \mathcal{N}, \mathcal{O}, \mathcal{L})$ consisting of a set of $I \in \mathcal{N}$ input sites, a set $\mathcal{N} \backslash \mathcal{I}$ of computing units, a set $\mathcal{O} \in \mathcal{N} \backslash \mathcal{I}$ of output sites, and a set $\mathcal{L}$ of links. A link is a tuple $(M, u, v, \overrightarrow{I}_2(u, v))$ whereby M is a 3-node A-type machine according to Figure 2.8, $u \in \mathcal{N}$ and $v \in \mathcal{N} \backslash \mathcal{I}$, $I[1](u, v) \in \{0, 1\}$ and $I[2](u, v) \in \{0, 1\}$ are the two interfering inputs. An input site $r \in \mathcal{I}$ has the value $x_r \in \{0, 1\}$ at the moment t, where $x_r[t]$ is the input value of x_r at the moment $t - 1$. The net input into unit $r \in \mathcal{N} \backslash \mathcal{I}$ at the moment t, $net(r, t)$, is the product

of the state $i(r) \in \mathcal{N}\backslash\mathcal{I}$ at $t-1$ and the state of $j(r) \in \mathcal{N}\backslash\mathcal{I}$ at $t-1$. The state $r \in \mathcal{N}\backslash\mathcal{I}$ at t is $1 - net(r,t)$ ∎

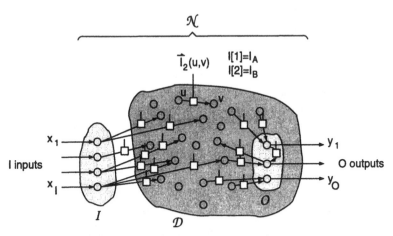

Fig. 2.19. Structure of a BI-type unorganized machine with inputs and outputs. Each link can be considered as a sort of dynamic switch that is either enabled (the signal passes) or disabled (the signal is interrupted and a 1 is on the link's output). The state of the switch can be modified by means of two interfering inputs I_A and I_B assigned to each link.

Definition 2.3.16 (BI-type neuron output)

Figure 2.20(a) shows that the output $d_n[t+1]$ of a unit n at time $t+1$ depends on the previous outputs of the units $d_i[t], i \in 1, ..., N$, $d_j[t], j \in 1, ..., N$ connected as inputs to unit d_n, on the internal state of the BI-type links, and on the interfering inputs $\overrightarrow{I}_2(i,n)$ and $\overrightarrow{I}_2(j,n)$. $l_{in}[t]$ and $l_{jn}[t]$ are calculated by Equation 2.31. ∎

$$d_n[t+1] = \begin{cases} x_n[t] & \text{if } n \in \mathcal{I} \\ f(l_{in}[t], \, l_{jn}[t]) & \text{if } n \in \mathcal{D}, \ i = 1, ..., N, \ j = 1, ..., N \end{cases}$$

$$= \begin{cases} x_n[t] & \text{if } n \in \mathcal{I} \\ 1 - l_{in}[t] \, l_{jn}[t] & \text{if } n \in \mathcal{D}, \ i = 1, ..., N, \ j = 1, ..., N \end{cases} \tag{2.32}$$

2.3.6 The B-type Pitfall

Remember the following statement already seen in Section 2.2.4:

"[...] that with suitable initial conditions they [i.e., B-type machines] will do any required job, given sufficient time and provided

(a)   (b)

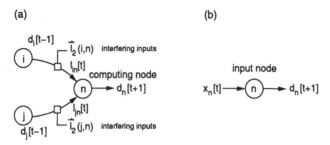

Fig. 2.20. Definition of the output $d_n[t+1]$ of a BI-type neuron n. The output of a computing node (a) depends on its two inputs $l_{in}[t]$ and $l_{jn}[t]$ whereas the output of an input node only depends on its direct input $x_n[t]$ (b).

the number of units is sufficient. In particular with a B-type unorganized machine with sufficient units one can find initial conditions which will make it into a universal machine with a given storage capacity" [192, p. 15].

Unfortunately, Turing made a silly mistake in the definition of his B-type machines that prevents the construction of a universal B-type machine. As it is well-known, AND and OR gates cannot be combined to produce all logical functions of n variables. The reader may try to implement the negation (NOT) as a combination of AND and OR gates. On the other hand, the following proposition holds:

Proposition 2.3.1 (Logical basis formed by NAND gates)
All logical functions can be implemented with a network of units that compute NAND functions. NAND gates thus form a logical basis.   ∎

A network of AND, OR, and NOT units is also able to compute all logical functions and thus forms another logical basis. This is easy to proof: it suffices to show that AND, OR, and NOT units can be realized by means of NAND units. Other logical basis exist: John von Neumann [203] showed that through a redundant coding of the inputs (each variable is transmitted through two lines) AND and OR units alone can constitute a logical basis as well.

To illustrate the above proposition, let us build up a Turing node only from NAND gates. Remember the illustration of the Turing node by a D flip-flop in Figure 2.3. The associated functional table is presented in Figure 2.4. A positive-edge-triggered D flip-flop samples its D input and changes its Q output only on the rising clock edge. Figure 2.21 shows how a Turing node can be replaced by NAND gates only. It is important to note that the resulting figure cannot be regarded as an A-type network. A Turing node is not just a NAND gate! The D flip-flop is absolutely necessary, otherwise one will get a completely asynchronous system where no central clock orchestrates the node's functioning.

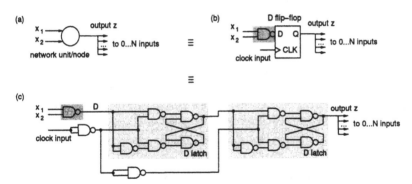

Fig. 2.21. To illustrate the universality of NAND gates, a Turing node (a)—a positive-edge-triggered D flip-flop with a preceding NAND gate (b)—is built up by NAND gates only (c).

Let us now come back to the mysteries of B-type networks. Figure 2.22(a) shows the smallest possible functional unit of a B-type network: one node with two B-type links. Suppose now that both links are enabled/closed and thus simply invert the signal. When abstracting from the delay of one clock cycle due to the D flip-flop in the link, the drawing of Figure 2.22(a) can be replaced by the drawing of Figure 2.22(b). The case when one or both links are disabled/opened (they have a 1 on their output and interrupt the signal) is uninteresting since this corresponds to an interrupted connection. The signals i and j are inverted and fed into the NAND gate of node n. Equation 2.33 shows that a B-type node together with its two associated input links is nothing more than a simple OR gate (Figure 2.22(c)), again, when abstracting from the D flip-flop delays!

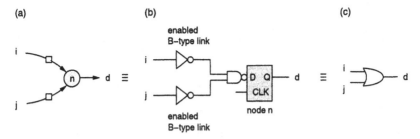

Fig. 2.22. Functional description of the smallest unit of B-type network: (a) one node with two B-type links. Drawing (a) can be replaced by drawing (b) when abstracting from the link delays. Drawing (c) shows the resulting function: an OR gate.

$$d = NAND(NOT(i), NOT(i)) = \overline{\overline{i}\,\overline{j}}$$
$$= i + j \qquad \text{(De Morgan)} \qquad (2.33)$$
$$= OR(i, j)$$

Since OR gates do not form a logical basis, it is now obvious that not all logical functions can be computed by Turing's B-type machines. To feel the difficulty, the reader may attempt to design a B-type network that computes the XOR or the NOT function!

Corollary 2.3.17 (The B-type disaster)
Turing's hypothesis stating that "[...] with suitable initial conditions they [i.e., B-type machines] will do any required job, given sufficient time and provided the number of units is sufficient" [192, p. 15] is wrong.   ∎

The same corollary is also valid for Bl-type machines, however not for A-type machines, as we shall see in Chapter 3. In addition, we shall see towards the end of the book (Section 5.2) more details on the computational power of Turing's unorganized machines in general.

2.4 New Unorganized Machines

In the previous section we have seen that B-type and Bl-type unorganized machines are not universal since Turing made a rather silly mistake in their definition. Because they cannot compute any logical function, there might be some serious limitations when applying B-type or Bl-type networks to real world problems.

This section shall present some new and universal machines. It is important to note that the machines presented in this section have *no* basis in Turing's writings! They are extensions and improvements of Turing's proposals.

2.4.1 CP-type Unorganized Machines

In their 1996 paper, Copeland and Proudfoot propose "[t]he simplest remedy [...]" [39] in the form of the following B-type link modification:

"[...] every unit-to-unit connection within an A-type machine is replaced by two of the devices [i.e., B-type links] [...] linked in series".

Figure 2.23(a) and shows this new kind of link which has been named CP-type link by the author. In analogy with the symbolic representation used by Turing for B-type links, the author proposed the symbol as seen in Figure 2.23(b). Each CP-type link simply consists of two B-type links that double inverse signals passing through the link. For a correct operation, it must be

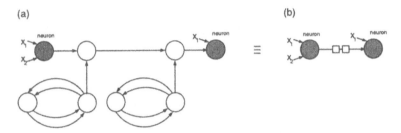

Fig. 2.23. The CP-type link proposed by Copeland and Proudfoot: it consists of two B-type links, the first one used as an inverter. To the right, symbolic representation proposed by the author.

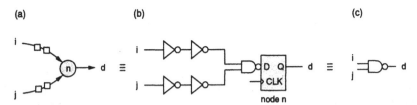

Fig. 2.24. Functional description of the smallest unit of a CP-type network: (a) one node with two CP-type links. Drawing (a) can be replaced by drawing (b) when abstracting from the link delays. Drawing (c) shows the resulting function: a NAND gate. CP-type networks are thus universal in the sense that they can compute any logical function.

assured that the first B-type link within the CP-type link is configured as inverter, i.e., that the link is enabled (closed).

Figure 2.23(a) shows the smallest possible functional unit of a CP-type network: one node with two CP-type links. Suppose now that both links are enabled/closed and thus simply invert the signal. When abstracting from the delay of one clock cycle due to the D flip-flop in the link, the drawing of Figure 2.23(a) can be replaced by the drawing of Figure 2.23(b). The case when one or both links are disabled/opened (they have a 1 on their output and interrupt the signal) is uninteresting since this corresponds to an interrupted connection. The signals i and j are inverted and fed into the NAND gate of node n. Equation 2.34 shows that a CP-type node together with its two associated input links is functionally equivalent to a NAND gate (Figure 2.23(c)), again, when neglecting the D flip-flop delays!

$$d = NAND(NOT(NOT(i)), NOT(NOT(j))) = \overline{\overline{\overline{i}}\,\overline{\overline{j}}}$$
$$= \overline{ab} \qquad\qquad (2.34)$$
$$= NAND(i, j)$$

A CP-type machine is thus defined as follows:

Definition 2.4.1 (CP-type machine)

A CP-*type machine is an* A-*type machine where each connection has been replaced by two* B-*type links in series.* ∎

Since a B-type link is itself a small A-type machine, a CP-type machine can be considered as an A-type machine that has been constructed in a particular way. The inverse statement is not valid in general as not all A-type machines are CP-type machines.

Similar to BI-type networks, one could easily imagine adding interfering inputs to a CP-type link in order to change its internal state (see also Section 2.2.3). The first B-type link is best used as an inverter only (without interfering inputs) and thus has to be set in an enabled (closed) state.

2.4.2 TB-type Unorganized Machines

Everyone who has once ran simulations of large neural networks or has implemented networks in hardware should know that speed and limited resources are critical values. Having two B-type links in series in each interconnection adds useless nodes and interconnections to the network. A simplification can easily be made: the author proposes the TB-type link as shown in Figure 2.25 that is functionally equivalent to a CP-type link, but simpler. Instead of a second B-type link, this link only uses a simple node that inverts the signal before it enters into the remaining B-type link.

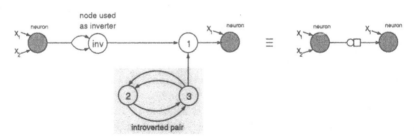

Fig. 2.25. The TB-type link proposed by Teuscher. A simple node is used as an inverter in series with a normal B-type link. The symbolic representation has also been proposed by the author.

A TB-type machine is thus defined as follows:

Definition 2.4.2 (TB-type machine)

A TB-*type machine is an* A-*type machine where each connection has been replaced by an additional* A-*type node in series with a* B-*type link as presented in Figure 2.25.* ∎

As previously seen with CP-type networks, a TB-type network also offers universal computational capabilities. This kind of machine will only have one small further application in the present book and we are thus not going to formalize and analyze it. The interested reader might be able to adapt without difficulty to formulations used for B-type networks in Sections 2.3.2 and 2.3.3.

2.4.3 TBI-type Unorganized Machines

Next, we need a modifiable and trainable machine built up from elements that form a logical basis and that allow the machine to compute any logical function. Similar to the step we made from B-type networks to BI-type networks, we add two interfering inputs to a TB-type link. The resulting link is called a TBI-type link and is shown in Figure 2.26.

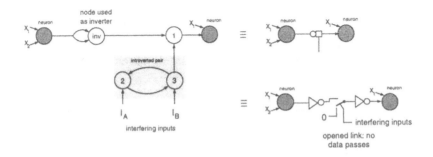

Fig. 2.26. TBI-type link and symbolic representation proposed by the author with two interfering inputs I_A and I_B that affect the internal state of the interconnection switch. The inverter-node that precedes the switch makes TBI-type networks universal.

Figure 2.27 shows the representation of a TBI-type link in the form of a sequential digital system. Since the introverted pair has not changed, the same state diagram as deduced for BI-type links (Section 2.3.4, Figure 2.18) remains valid. The state of the link can be changed by applying appropriate signals to I_A and I_B. Figure 2.28 shows the notation used for representing the actual state of a link. The same representation can also be used for B-type, CP-type, or TB-type links.

We are now ready to define a TBI-type machine:

Definition 2.4.3 (TBI-type machine)
A TBI-type machine is an A-type machine where each connection has been replaced by a TBI-type link as shown in Figure 2.27. ∎

The structure of a TBI-type unorganized machine is depicted in Figure 2.29. In lieu of a mathematical formulation as it has been made in Section 2.3 for Turing's original networks, a TBI-type network simulation in MATLAB will be presented in Section 2.5.

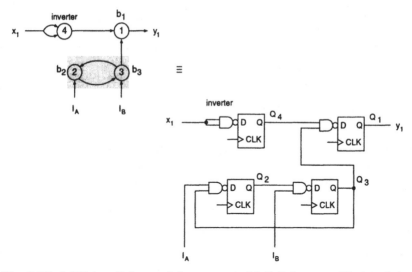

Fig. 2.27. A TBI-type link regarded as a sequential digital system. The interfering inputs I_A and I_B are used to change the state of the link.

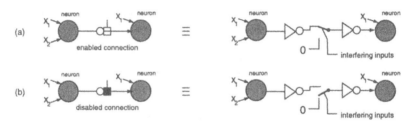

Fig. 2.28. Representation of the state of a link. (a) shows an enabled/closed link, (b) a disabled/opened one.

2.4.4 BS-type Unorganized Machines

All links with interfering inputs we have seen so far contain one or even two D flip-flops in the signal data-path. Each flip-flop adds an additional one-clock-cycle delay to the signal that passes through the interconnection switch. Besides the beauty of building up networks with all and the same components (A-type nodes), there is no real advantage of using several D flip-flops to build up a switch. A major drawback of delay units within interconnections is the difficulty to meet timing constraints and to synchronize signals in larger networks.

There exists a digital component that exactly meets the specification of links with interfering inputs: the *multiplexer* [206]. Figure 2.30 is a possible realization of a new type of link, called a BS-type link. A multiplexer is used to enable or disable the link. A 1 on the interfering input I selects the input coming from the source neuron, $I = 0$ disables the interconnection and puts

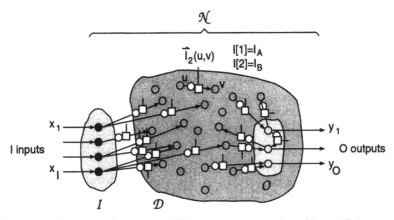

Fig. 2.29. Structure of a universal TBl-type unorganized machine with inputs and outputs. Each link can be considered as a sort of dynamic switch that is either enabled (the signal passes) or disabled (the signal is interrupted and a 1 is on the link's output). The state of the switch can be modified by means of two interfering inputs I_A and I_B.

a constant 1 on the destination node. The downside of this kind of link is that it has no internal memory storing its state. Note that the BS-type link also allows the construction of networks that have universal computational capabilities.

These kind of machines will have further applications in the examples of Chapter 4: firstly they do not need as many resources as TBl-type networks; secondly the signal propagation time is much shorter, thus, allowing for faster and larger network simulations. Turing's B-type networks are networks with nodes and interconnections that can be enabled or disabled. At least functionally, a BS-type network respects Turing's main ideas, however, a BS-type network is not built up from all and the same primitive elements.

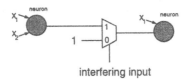

Fig. 2.30. BS-type link with interfering input I proposed by the author. A multiplexer is used to enable or disable the link. A 1 on the interfering input I selects the input coming from the source neuron, $I = 0$ selects and disables the interconnection and puts a constant 1 on the destination node.

2.4.5 Bl1-type Link

Another simplification might be useful: reducing the two interfering inputs to one. The two meta stable states S_0 and S_3 (see Table 2.3) can be removed without any loss of functionality. The following simplification is made:

$$I_A = \overline{I_B}. \tag{2.35}$$

This requires an additional inverter in the link that generates I_B from I_A. Figure 2.31 shows a possible implementation in the form of a sequential digital system. The link is called a Bl1-type link. Since an additional element—the inverter—is necessary, the network is no longer homogeneous and built up from "standard" elements. However, control for organizing the machine might be reduced as there is only one instead of two interfering inputs per connection.

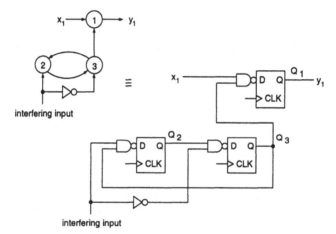

Fig. 2.31. Bl1-type link: Bl-type link with one interfering input I. An additional inverter is necessary.

This kind of machine will have no further application in the present book.

2.5 Simulation of TBI-type Machines with **MATLAB**

2.5.1 MATLAB

MATLAB[2] is a language for technical computing and visualization. Its basic data element is the matrix (the name MATLAB stands for matrix laboratory) that does not require a dimension. MATLAB features a family of application-specific solutions called toolboxes. Toolboxes are collections of MATLAB functions (M-files) that extend the MATLAB environment to solve particular classes of problems. Areas in which toolboxes are available include signal processing, control systems, neural networks, fuzzy logic, wavelets, simulation, and many others.

Modelling neural networks in MATLAB is certainly not the best choice if you are only interested in powerful simulations. MATLAB is principally an interpreted language that is not as powerful as compiled code. It also offers the possibility of compilation, but with limited improvement in performance. Advantages of MATLAB include the simplicity of usage, the flexibility, and the enormous number of already integrated functions for simulation and visualization.

In this section, we shall see how TBI-type networks might be implemented and simulated in MATLAB. A very simple and illustrative toolbox will be presented that is also available online [176]. Note that the implementation shown below represents one of many possible examples. This section should also help non-scientists working with Turing networks. For those who are not familiar with MATLAB, take a look at the MathWorks web-site[3] where many manuals are available online or in pdf-format. If this is not sufficient, a wide range of books about MATLAB is available in almost any scientific bookstore.

2.5.2 A Simple TBI-type **MATLAB** Toolbox

In lieu of a connection matrix as presented for A-type and B-type networks, we use a different approach for TBI-type networks. Connections and associated internal connection values are represented in one and the same matrix. The matrix—the heart of MATLAB and the TBI-type simulation—has the following format:

Definition 2.5.1 (TBI-type network link matrix)

$$
C_{L \times 6} = \begin{bmatrix} link_1 \\ \vdots \\ link_L \end{bmatrix} = \begin{bmatrix} from & to & inverter & node_1 & node_2 & node_3 \\ \vdots & \vdots & \vdots & \vdots & \vdots & \vdots \\ from & to & inverter & node_1 & node_2 & node_3 \end{bmatrix} \quad (2.36) \quad \blacksquare
$$

---

[2] MATLAB is a registered trademark of The MathWorks, Inc.
[3] http://www.mathworks.com.

Nodes are numbered from 1 to L. Any node receives inputs from exactly two other nodes. The internal link nodes (*inverter*, *node 1*, *node 2*, and *node 3*) are numbered according to Figure 2.27. The generation of the network link matrix has been separated in two different functions. First, function randllist randomly generates a $L \times 2$ matrix that only contains source and destination of all links. In a second step, randswstates randomly generates a $L \times 4$ matrix that contains the internal link states of all links. Function randswstates further calls function randswstate to generate the state of a single introverted pair.

```
function[result]=randllist(ninputs,nnodes)

%RANDLLIST    Generates a link list
%    RANDLLIST generates a random link
%    list [from to] with two connections
%    per node (k=2).

llist=[];
for n=ninputs+1:nnodes
    % Find two random source nodes
    source1=round(rand*(nnodes-1)+1);
    source2=round(rand*(nnodes-1)+1);
    llist=[llist; [source1 n]];
    llist=[llist; [source2 n]];
end
result=llist;
```

```
function[result]=randswstates(nlinks)

%RANDSWSTATES    Returns TBI-type links state matrix
%    RANDSWSTATES(nlinks) returns a TBI-type link
%    state matrix according to the following format:
%
%    [inverter node1 node2 node3]    link 1
%                ...
%    [inverter node1 node2 node3]    link <NLINKS>

switches=[];
for l=1:nlinks;
    switches=[switches;randswstate];
end
result=[round(rand(nlinks,2)),switches];
```

```
function[result]=randswstate()

%RANDSWSTATE    Random switch state
%    RANDSWSTATE returns a randomly initialised
%    switch state (open or closed).

s2=round(rand);
if s2==1
    s3=0;    % opened/disabled switch
else
    s3=1;    % closed/enabled switch
end
result=[s2,s3];
```

In the following, several examples will demonstrate the usage of some functions.

Example 2.5.1 (TBl-type network link matrix)

A random link state matrix is generated in the present example. The network consists of eight nodes, two input nodes, and 12 links.

```
>> nnodes=8

nnodes =

     8

>> ninputs=2

ninputs =

     2

>> nlinks=13

nlinks =

    12

>> llist=randllist(ninputs,nnodes)

llist =

     1     3
     4     3
     1     4
     1     4
```

```
    4    5
    6    5
    2    6
    7    6
    5    7
    8    7
    3    8
    7    8
```

```
>> lstates=randswstates(nlinks)
```

lstates =

```
    0    1    1    0
    1    0    1    0
    1    0    0    1
    0    0    1    0
    1    0    0    1
    1    1    0    1
    1    1    0    1
    1    0    0    1
    0    1    0    1
    1    0    1    0
    1    1    1    0
    1    1    0    1
```

```
>> lmat=[llist lstates]
```

lmat =

```
    1    3    0    1    1    0
    4    3    1    0    1    0
    1    4    1    0    0    1
    1    4    0    0    1    0
    4    5    1    0    0    1
    6    5    1    1    0    1
    2    6    1    1    0    1
    7    6    1    0    0    1
    5    7    0    1    0    1
    8    7    1    0    1    0
    3    8    1    1    1    0
    7    8    1    1    0    1
```

The reader is invited to draw the network starting from the link state matrix lmat. *Figure 2.32 shows the result. Initial values (at time $t = 0$) are printed beside each node.*

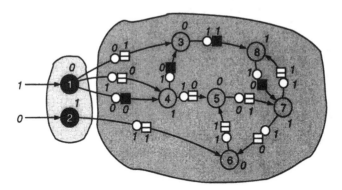

Fig. 2.32. Randomly generated TBI-type network according to the link state matrix lmat. Initial node values and initial internal link values are written beside the nodes.

The function randvec simply returns a randomly generated binary vector of dimension dim:

```
function[result]=randvec(dim)

%RANDVEC   Returns a binary random vector
%   <DIM> dimension of the random vector

result=round(rand(dim,1));
```

The main function that randomly generates a TBI-type network and that runs it for T time steps is called tbiruns. The function takes the following arguments: the number of simulation steps, the number of input nodes, and the total number of nodes.

```
function[result]=tbiruns(nsteps,ninputs,nnodes)

%TBIRUNS   Runs a TBI-type net for <nsteps>
%   <NSTEPS> is the number of simulation steps,
%   <NINPUTS> the number of input nodes, and
%   <NNODES> the total number of network nodes.

% Generate random link list
% [from to]
llist=randllist(ninputs,nnodes);
nlinks=length(llist);

% Generate random link state matrix
% [inv n1 n2 n3]
lstates=randswstates(nlinks);

% Compose link matrix
% [from to inv n1 n2 n3]
lmat=[llist lstates];

% Generate random state vector
statevec=randvec(nnodes);
history=statevec;

% Generate random input_vector
ivec=randvec(ninputs);

for steps=1:nsteps
   % Save link outputs
   lostates=lmat(:,4);
   % For all links propagate data
   for l=1:nlinks
      % Update link l
      % n1=inv NAND n3
      lmat(l,4)=1-lmat(l,3)*lmat(l,6);
      % inv=new link input value
      lmat(l,3)=1-statevec(lmat(l,1));
      n2old=lmat(l,5);
      % n2=n3 NAND n3
      lmat(l,5)=1-lmat(l,6);
      % n3=n2 NAND n2
      lmat(l,6)=1-n2old;
   end
   % Generate new state vector
   statevec=gennewstate(nnodes,nlinks,ivec,lostates,lmat);
   history=[history statevec];
end
result=history;
```

First, a link matrix lmat, a random state vector statevec as well as a random input vector ivec are generated. The main loop (for steps=1:nsteps) then propagates data in each link and generates the new state vector by means of the function gennewstate. This function simply performs a NAND operation between all incoming links of a given node.

Furthermore, tbiruns holds a trace of all state vectors during simulation in the variable history. This history will be returned by the function.

```
function[result]=gennewstate(nnodes,nlinks,ivec,lostates,lmat)

%GENNEWSTATE    Generates state vector
%    GENNEWSTATE generates the state vector
%    from the link matrix <LMAT>.

nstatevec=ivec;
% For each node, determine the incoming links
for n=length(ivec)+1:nnodes
    inputs=[];
    % For all links in lmat
    for l=1:nlinks
        % lmat: [from to inv n1 n2 n3]
        % Look for incoming links for node n
        if lmat(l,2)==n
            % Save values of incoming links in
            % <inputs>
            inputs=[inputs; lostates(l)];
        end
    end
    % NAND operation on all incoming links
    nstatevec=[nstatevec; 1-prod(inputs)];
end
result=nstatevec;
```

Example 2.5.2 (TBI-type network simulation)

Suppose our function tbiruns *has generated initial settings according to Example 2.5.1. Called with the argument* steps = 10, *it would thus return the following state vector history:*

```
>> tbiruns(10,2,8)

ans =

     0    1    1    1    1    1    1    1    1    1    1
     1    0    0    0    0    0    0    0    0    0    0
     0    1    0    0    0    0    0    0    0    0    0
     1    1    1    1    0    0    0    0    0    0    0
     0    1    1    1    0    0    1    1    1    1    1
     0    1    1    0    1    1    1    1    1    1    1
     1    1    0    1    0    0    0    1    1    0    0
     1    0    1    0    0    1    0    1    1    1    0
```

Figure 2.33 shows the new node values (after one clock cycle) of the network presented in Figure 2.32. One can see that the second column of the above matrix corresponds to the state of the network nodes.

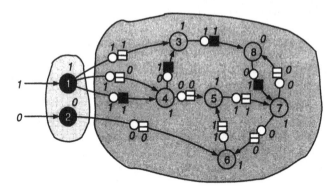

Fig. 2.33. Representation of the network values resulting from a one clock simulation of the randomly generated network of Figure 2.32.

The interested reader should be able to extend the MATLAB toolbox presented in this section without too many problems.

3. Synthesis of Logical Functions and Digital Systems with Turing Networks

Computers are composed of nothing more than logic gates stretched out to the horizon in a vast numerical irrigation system.
— Stan Augarten, *State of the Art: A Photographic History of the Integrated Circuit*, 1983.

This chapter deals with the synthesis of basic logical functions and simple digital systems by means of unorganized machines. A digital system normally uses a building block approach: many small operational units are interconnected to make up the overall system. Logical functions (gates) like conjunction (AND), disjunction (OR), and negation (NOT) form the basis of every logical and digital system. As we have already seen in Section 2.3.6, all logical functions can be implemented with a network of units that compute NAND functions. We say that NAND gates form a logical basis.

Historically, the high voltage or more positive voltage level was associated with binary 1 while low voltage or less positive level was associated with binary 0. If this choice is adhered to throughout an entire system of logic gates, it is called a *positive logic system* [33]. This is currently the case for all the elements and systems presented in this book.

The present chapter does not deal with randomly generated machines. Most of the machines are designed and optimized for a given task. Machine organization—as Turing imagined (by means of enabling and disabling connection switches)—is not considered in this chapter. One might say that the machines are already in an organized form. Evolution and organization of unorganized machines will be discussed in Chapter 4.

No expert knowledge about digital systems is assumed for this chapter. Readers that are unfamiliar with switching algebra and digital systems design might take a look at Wakerly [206].

3.1 Combinational versus Sequential Systems

A circuit or system is called *combinational* if it depends only on the current input combination. It is called *sequential* if it contains flip-flops and thus depends not only on the inputs but also on the past sequence of inputs that have been applied. In other words, a sequential system has a *memory* of past events [206]. A combinational circuit may contain an arbitrary number of logic gates but no feedback loops—at least in a conventional combinational circuit.

The mindful reader has already realized that Turing's unorganized machines are sequential systems since each node contains a flip-flop with a preceding NAND gate. Even though the networks contain flip-flops, they can still be used to compute combinational logical functions. We simply assume that the clock frequency of the sequential system is sufficiently high compared to the changes of the system's input signals. This assumption can be compared to the specifications of a real logical gate where each signal is propagated with a certain *propagation delay* through the gate. Even though this delay is some nanoseconds only, it has to be considered when building digital systems.

3.2 Synthesis of Logical Functions with A-type Networks

In this section we shall see that it is possible to implement any logical function with an A-type network. We shall also see that this might be very tricky. The implementation of state machines will be discussed in Section 5.3. In the following, the elemental logical functions are described and illustrated by an implementation.

The reader can easily see that the logical function computed by an A-type node is the NAND operation since each node contains one two-input NAND gate followed by a D flip-flop (see also Figure 2.3). In order to realize other logical functions, they have thus to be built up on NAND functions—which, as we have seen in Section 2.3.6, is always possible. Yet, we already know from a theoretical point of view that A-type networks are universal. Nonetheless, let us see how things work in reality.

The basic logical operators are defined as follows:

- A *NOT* gate, usually called an *inverter*, produces an output value that is the opposite of its input value.
- An *AND* gate produces a 1 if and only if all of its inputs are 1.
- An *OR* gate produces a 1 if and only if one or more of its inputs are 1.
- An *NAND* gate produces the opposite of an AND gate's output, a 0 if and only if all of its inputs are 1.
- An *Exclusive* OR (*XOR*) gate is a two-input gate whose output is 1 if and only if exactly one of its inputs is 1.

The next step consists in describing the above logical functions using only NAND functions. Equations 3.1, 3.2, 3.3, and 3.4 show how this could be done for NOT, AND, OR, and XOR functions. For more details about these transformations see for example Wakerly [206].

$$NOT(a) = \bar{a}$$
$$= NOT(AND(a,a)) \tag{3.1}$$
$$= NAND(a,a)$$

$$AND(a,b) = ab = \overline{\overline{ab}}$$
$$= NOT(NAND(a,b)) \tag{3.2}$$
$$= NAND(NAND(a,b), NAND(a,b))$$

$$OR(a,b) = a + b = \overline{\bar{a}\bar{b}}$$
$$= NAND(NOT(a), NOT(b)) \tag{3.3}$$
$$= NAND(NAND(a,a), NAND(b,b))$$

$$XOR(a,b) = a \oplus b = \bar{a}b + a\bar{b}$$
$$= \overline{\overline{\bar{a}b}\,\overline{a\bar{b}}}$$
$$= NAND(NAND(NOT(a),b),$$
$$NAND(a, NOT(b))) \tag{3.4}$$
$$= NAND(NAND(NAND(a,a),b),$$
$$NAND(a, NAND(b,b)))$$

The last step simply consists of implementing the above equations using A-type nodes. Thereby, each NAND function directly corresponds to an A-type neuron. In addition, an input node (D flip-flop) has been added for each input signal. For better understanding, Figure 3.1 shows the realization of a NAND function by means of an A-type network. This is trivial since it only needs one A-type node (besides the two input nodes). All figures (3.1, 3.2, 3.3, 3.4, and 3.5) also show a timing diagram. CLK is the global clock signal for all network nodes. NOT, AND, and OR functions only require a stable input for one clock cycle. On the other hand, the XOR gate (Figure 3.5) requires a stable input signal for two clock cycles since the input signal is used by the first and the second network layer. Depending on the number of network layers, the results need several clock cycles to be valid on the network output. The reader may already sense the upcoming difficulty in the construction of larger systems: to keep within all timing constraints can become really tricky!

So far, we have seen that basic logical functions can be implemented by means of A-type nodes. From Proposition 2.3.1 we know that NAND gates form a logical basis. Another logical basis is formed by AND, OR, and NOT functions. Thus, the following proposition (3.2.1) holds:

Proposition 3.2.1 (Logical functions with A-type networks)
Every logical function can be computed by an A-type network.   ∎

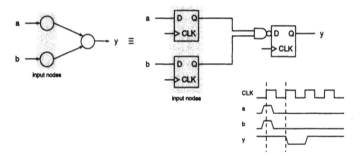

Fig. 3.1. Two-input NAND function realized by an A-type network. Only one A-type node is needed.

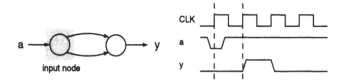

Fig. 3.2. NOT function realized by an A-type network.

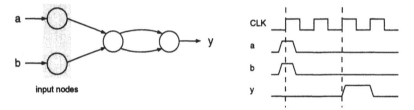

Fig. 3.3. Two-input AND function realized by an A-type network.

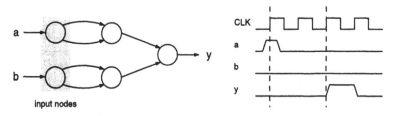

Fig. 3.4. Two-input OR function realized by an A-type network.

What was proven wrong for B-type networks (see Section 2.3.6) is true for A-type networks: A-type networks *are* universal machines. Note that the above proposition says nothing about the complexity of an eventual realization. The implementation of complex logical functions with lots of variables can certainly be very tricky.

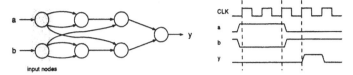

Fig. 3.5. Two-input XOR function realized by an A-type network. The two inputs must be stable for two clock cycles as they are used by the first and second network layer.

3.3 Synthesis of Logical Functions with TB-type Networks

In the previous section we have seen that all logical functions can be implemented by A-type networks. For AND, OR, NOT, NAND, and XOR functions a possible implementation has been given. As seen in Section 2.4.2, TB-type networks are A-type networks with special interconnections. We also know that they are universal and that they can thus compute any logical function. While working with TB-type networks, one has to be aware of the additional two-clock delay due to the D flip-flops within the interconnections. It will thus be more difficult to satisfy the timing constraints of larger networks. In general, all interconnections must be in an enabled state. We use the notation as presented in Figure 2.28. TBI-type networks are not especially mentioned in this section, but all designs and properties are also valid for them. One must be careful that interfering inputs are set and that the interconnections are enabled.

For illustrative purposes, Figures 3.6, 3.7, 3.8, 3.9, and 3.10 show possible implementations of AND, OR, NOT, NAND, and XOR functions using TB-type nodes. As one can see, the networks are identical to the machines of the previous section (with the exception of the type of link used), however, the timings are different: a signal needs much more time to get through a network.

Exactly like for A-type networks, the following proposition holds:

Proposition 3.3.1 (Logical functions with TB-type networks)
Every logical function can be computed by a TB-type network.   ∎

3.4 Multiplexer and Demultiplexer

Multiplexer and demultiplexer [206] are elements that are widely used in digital systems. A *multiplexer* is a digital switch—it connects data from one of n sources to its output. A *demultiplexer* is the inverse of a multiplexer. A 1-bit, n-output demultiplexer has one data input and n data outputs. All outputs except the selected one are 0. The selected output equals the data

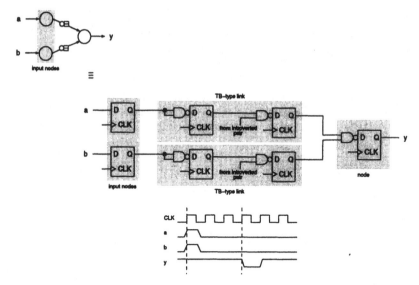

Fig. 3.6. Two-input NAND function realized by a TB-type network.

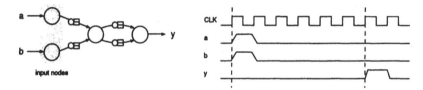

Fig. 3.7. Two-input AND function realized by a TB-type network.

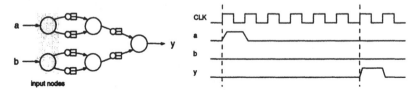

Fig. 3.8. Two-input OR function realized by a TB-type network.

input. Figure 3.11 shows a four-input multiplexer, Figure 3.12 a four-output demultiplexer.

As one can see, the above diagrams contain three- and four-input AND gates as well as inverters. However, they can easily be transformed into diagrams that only use NAND gates as internal building blocks. Figure 3.13 depicts a four-input multiplexer implementation based on NAND gates only.

It is not too difficult to build up a three- or four-input NAND gate from TB-type nodes: Figure 3.14 shows a possible implementation of a three-input gate. According to the notation presented in Figure 2.28, connections drawn

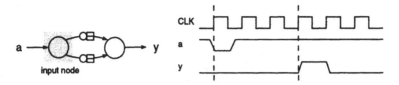

Fig. 3.9. NOT function realized by a TB-type network with input nodes.

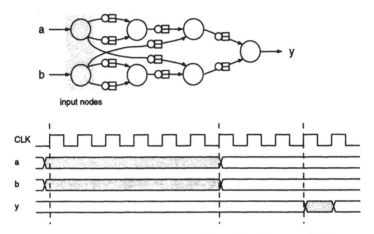

Fig. 3.10. Two-input XOR function realized by a TB-type network. The two inputs must be stable for six clock cycles.

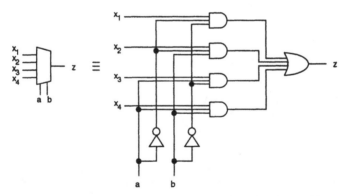

Fig. 3.11. Four-input multiplexer block-diagram symbol and possible implementation.

with a black rectangular box always have a 1 on their output (disabled connections). The reader is invited to design a four-input multiplexer on its own (a possible solution might be found in Figure 3.15). An inverter has already been implemented in the previous section, however, a slightly different version will be used.

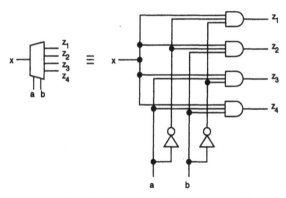

Fig. 3.12. Four-output demultiplexer block-diagram symbol and possible implementation.

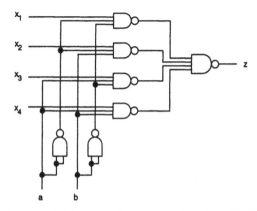

Fig. 3.13. Four-input multiplexer implementation based on NAND gates only.

Thus, the basic building blocks are now ready to be assembled to a TB-type multiplexer. Figure 3.15 shows the complete four-input multiplexer TB-type network. One can see on the timing diagram (see Figure 3.16) that the inputs must be valid at the latest three clock cycles after the control signals a and b are valid in order to guarantee a correct result on clock cycle 21. Furthermore, the control signals a and b must be stable for at least three clock cycles because of the two inverters.

Designing a demultiplexer is even easier because no four-input NAND gate is needed. The interested reader might easily find a possible realization.

3.5 Delay-Unit

For signal synchronization in larger systems, a unit that delays data is often required. A *delay-unit* is a system that transmits signals with a delay of d

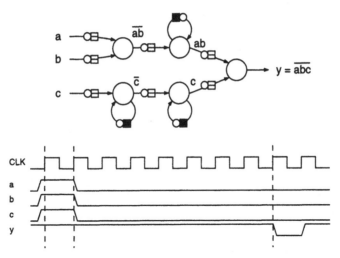

Fig. 3.14. 3-input NAND gate with TB-type network.

clock cycles. The smallest delay-unit that can be realized based on a TB-type network has a delay of three clock cycles (see Figure 3.17). Thus, the following proposition holds:

Proposition 3.5.1 (TB-type delay-units)
The delay of a TB-type delay-unit is always a multiple of three.   ∎

It is thus impossible to generate a delay of one clock cycle by a TB-type network. This would however be possible by means of an A-type machine, where the smallest delay is a one clock cycle (see Figure 3.18). As one can easily see, an A-type network can thus—in wiring the nodes in series—implement any required delay.

Proposition 3.5.2 (A-type delay-units)
Every delay can be realized by an A-type network.   ∎

In [192], Turing presented a randomly—at least he claimed—generated B-type machine that passes signals with a delay of four "moments". This machine is reproduced in Figure 3.19. For a randomly generated machine, the challenge consists in finding suitable initial link settings that let the machine perform its desired task. In most cases, there will be—because of disabled connections—many unused nodes in the system that could be removed without affecting the system's behaviour. Clearly, with regard to a manually designed system, a random machine is all but optimal because of the allocated, but unused resources.

Turing wrote that if connections 1, 3, 6, and 4 are initially disabled and connections 2, 5, and 7 enabled, then the machine passes signals with a delay of four clock cycles. One could see that node 3 is unused and that connection 2 could also be disabled. Other possible configurations might be easily found.

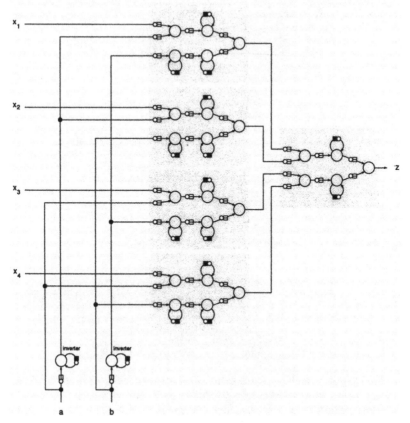

Fig. 3.15. TB-type network implementation of a four-input multiplexer.

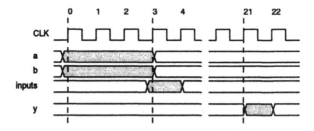

Fig. 3.16. Timing diagram of the above four-input TB-type multiplexer.

3.6 Shift-Register

Although a real implementation of a Turing machine is of no practical interest (the machine works very inefficiently!), the theoretical interest is to prove that a system can perform universal computations. Restrepo et al. [147] im-

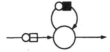

Fig. 3.17. The smallest delay unit that can be realized based on a TB-type network has a delay of three clock cycles.

Fig. 3.18. The smallest delay unit that can be built with an A-type network has a delay of one clock cycle (one D flip-flop).

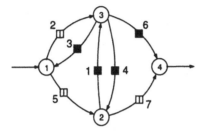

Fig. 3.19. Turing's B-type machine that passes signals with a delay of four clock cycles.

plemented a universal Turing machine on a cellular substrate. The clue they used to implement the machine is the following: instead of a fixed tape and a moving head they used a mobile tape—in the form of a bidirectional shift-register—and a fixed head. It is clear that a real tape can never be of infinite length, however, it can be made as long as desired (with respect to the physical constraints). The main interest of the presented shift-register implementation is to come closer to a possible realization of a universal Turing machine by means of TB-type nodes.

A shift-register is a n-bit register with a provision for shifting its stored data by one bit position on each clock [206]. The simplest shift-register is unidirectional and has just one serial input and one serial output. More complicated versions support bidirectional shifting, parallel input, and parallel output.

Figure 3.20 shows the structure of a bidirectional shift-register with parallel input and output. One segment has been drawn in detail. By assembling n segments in series, a n-bit shift register can easily be constructed.

In order to implement a shift-register built up from TB-type nodes, Figure 3.20 is best transformed in a system that only uses NAND gates. Figure 3.21 shows the result of this transformation. Note that only one shift-register segment is drawn. One can also see that the multiplexer of Figure 3.13 has been reused.

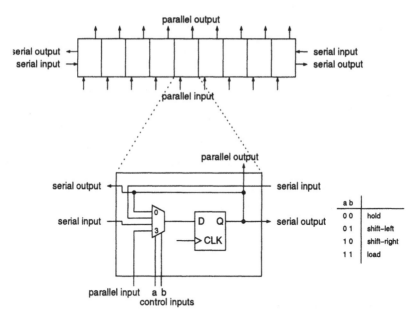

Fig. 3.20. Structure of a bidirectional shift-register with parallel input and output.

The next step consists of transforming Figure 3.21 into a TB-type network. The biggest part of that transformation—the multiplexer—has already been presented in Section 3.4. In fact, nothing more is needed as the multiplexer's output node (which contains a D flip-flop) might directly be used as D flip-flop of the shift-register segment. Figure 3.22 shows a possible implementation.

Figure 3.23 shows that 21 clock cycles are needed to process data within a shift-register. The inputs must be valid no later than three clocks after the control signals a and b in order to obtain a correct result. By assembling n segments as shown in Figure 3.22 in series, a n-bit TB-type shift register can easily be constructed.

The above shift-register implementation proves that a Turing machine tape can be implemented by means of a TB-type network. The control unit of a universal Turing machine can be described as a finite state machine (see Minsky [125] for more details). This, as it will be shown in Section 5.3, is not too much of a problem. The implementation of a universal Turing machine based on TB-type nodes has thus come within the bounds of possibility!

3.7 How to Design Complex Systems

Digital systems design is engineering, an art, and "problem solving" that requires a lot of creativity, although today many automated software tools are available. Hardware description languages (like VHDL or Verilog), cir-

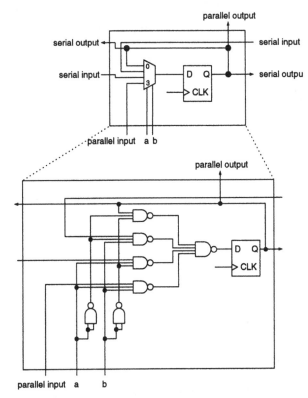

Fig. 3.21. Bidirectional shift-register implementation using NAND gates only.

cuit simulation, and circuit synthesis tools have radically changed the entire landscape of digital design. Designing complex digital systems is designing and understanding the basic functional blocks, and assembling these blocks together to make more and more complex blocks. It is a *building block* or, from a top-down point of view, a *divide-and-conquer* approach.

We have seen that any digital system can be described by means of NAND gates only. Even the most complex computer might be described by NAND gates only. Furthermore, we have seen in the previous sections how to implement simple digital components based on TB-type networks. The approach we used might roughly be summarized as follows:

1. Design the digital system in conventional logic (using AND, OR, NOT, etc. gates).
2. Transform it into a design that uses NAND gates only (this is always possible and can easily be automated).
3. Replace every NAND gate by a Turing network node.
4. Insert delay elements where necessary.

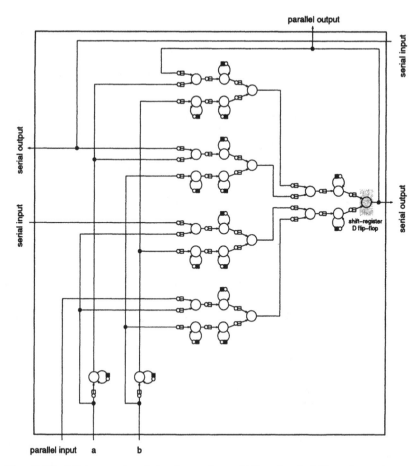

Fig. 3.22. TB-type network implementing a bidirectional shift-register segment with parallel input and output.

This will work well for smaller systems only. When assembling smaller blocks to form larger systems, further delay elements might be required between subsystems. In general, it will become more and more difficult to satisfy all timing constraints with increasing system size. However, this is not a fundamental problem, "only" an engineering one.

Finally, it has to be said that Turing did not seem particularly interested in the design of networks. Inspired by the human brain, he was much more fascinated by randomly constructed machines that could be organized in a certain manner to perform a desired task. The main goals of the present chapter were:

1. to illustrate how a Turing machine might be constructed by means of a Turing network and

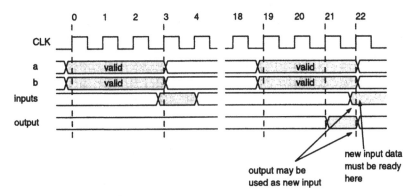

Fig. 3.23. Timing diagram of the TB-type shift-register.

2. to illustrate that every digital systems can be realized by an appropriate A-type, TB-type, or TBl-type network.

3.8 Hardware Implementation

Neural networks provide a challenge for the development of novel network implementations in hardware. The goal is to exploit the inherent massively parallel structure of neural networks and to carry out very fast neural computations. Thereby, binary neural networks (e.g., Turing neural networks) are particularly interesting models because of their neuron simplicity. Neural network hardware implementations have attracted increasing attention since the early 1990s with the advent of easily *reconfigurable hardware* such as *field programmable gate arrays* (FPGAs) [180]. In this context, the term *evolvable hardware* refers to hardware that can change its architecture and behaviour dynamically and autonomously by interacting with its environment. Often, evolutionary hardware uses an evolutionary algorithm for optimizing the systems topology and behaviour to an environment.

The first integrated neural networks were based on analog technology, with the advantage of speed and integration, but with significant disadvantages in terms of precision and sensitivity to noise and crosstalk. Digital implementations do not suffer the inherent drawbacks of analog circuits, as they allow arbitrary precision, strong noise immunity and easy interfacing to other system components. The main advantage of neural networks implemented in hardware is the speed-up with regard to conventional software simulations. Reconfigurable hardware can provide a very good combination of high-performance and flexibility. Today, FPGAs are competitive with *application specific integrated circuits* (ASICs) in terms of performance. They offer much more flexibility than ASICs, are cheaper, and easy to use. Most devices are reprogrammable or even partially reprogrammable. Furthermore, they can be classified into static and dynamic configurable systems [157].

Implementing classical neural networks in FPGAs can be rather complicated and resource consuming because of the multipliers usually needed for computing the neuron outputs. Stochastic bitstream coding (further presented in Section 4.4) presents already a major progress in simplifying the multiplications. Bade and Hutchings [17], for example, implemented a stochastic single layer network with 12 inputs and ten outputs on a Xilinx 4003 FPGA. Below, we will see that it is possible to put many more Turing neurons in an FPGA.

In the reminder of this section, a *VHDL* (high level hardware description language) implementation of Turing TBl-type networks will be described. Readers who are not familiar with VHDL and FPGAs might want to jump directly to the next section. VHDL is a popular high level hardware description language. Using dedicated compilers, simulators, and synthesis tools, a VHDL description is transferred into a configuration bitstream that is used to configure the reprogrammable circuit. A good introduction to VHDL can be found in [14]. Many resources are also available on the internet. A good starting point is the international VHDL home-page: http://www.vhdl.org.

The following two VHDL listings show the implementation of a D flip-flop and of a NAND gate, the two primitives of Turing neural networks:

```
entity dff is
  port (clk     : in   std_logic;
        reset   : in   std_logic;
        d       : in   std_logic;
        q       : out  std_logic);
end dff;

architecture synth of dff is
begin
  clocked : process (clk)
  begin
    if (clk'event and clk = '1') then
      if (reset = '1') then
        q <= '0';
      else
        q <= d;
      end if;
    end if;
  end process clocked;
end synth;
```

```
entity nand2 is
  port (a    : in  std_logic;
        b    : in  std_logic;
        z    : out std_logic);
end nand2;

architecture synth of nand2 is
begin
  z <= a NAND b;
end synth;
```

Note that I defend a "decompose-as-far-as-possible" strategy for VHDL designs. That is the reason why I even use a separate entity for a NAND gate. Be aware that VHDL, when used for synthesis, is a hardware description language and *not* a programming language in the conventional sense. Best synthesis results are obtained when, in a first step, a schematic drawing of the circuit is established. Then, all components and sub-systems are described and interconnected in VHDL. This seems idiotic, however, it gives wonderful results at synthesis! In doing so, the only advantage in respect to schematic drawing is that a VHDL design can be parameterized and that changes are thus often easier to realize.

Based on the NAND and D flip-flop described above, a Turing network node can now straightforwardly be described. One can see that the output of the NAND gate is connected to the input of the D flip-flop. The entity **node** has a clock input, a reset input, and the incoming connection inputs a and b. The node output is labeled with z.

```
entity node is
  port (clk    : in  std_logic;
        reset  : in  std_logic;
        a      : in  std_logic;
        b      : in  std_logic;
        z      : out std_logic);
end node;

architecture synth of node is
  signal nand_out   : std_logic;
begin
  comp_nand : nand2
    port map (a => a, b => b, z => nand_out);
  comp_dff : dff
    port map (clk => clk, reset => reset,
              d => nand_out, q => z);
end synth;
```

A TBl-type link is then simply an assembly of three **node** entities. The entity **tbi_links** looks as follows:

```
entity tbi_link is
  port (clk   : in  std_logic;
        reset : in  std_logic;
        a     : in  std_logic;
        i_a   : in  std_logic;
        i_b   : in  std_logic;
        z     : out std_logic);
end tbi_link;
```

The detailed code is not reproduced here but can be found on the book web-site (http://www.teuscher.ch/turing). The VHDL code contains only instances of the already existing **node** entity. Thus, the primitives of a TBI-type network are now realized in VHDL. A possible TBI-type network entity called **tbi_net** is shown in Figure 3.24.

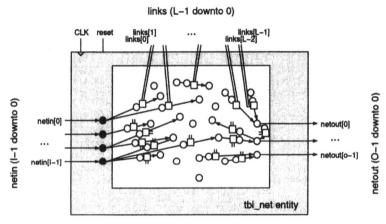

Fig. 3.24. Sample tbi_net entity realizing a complete TBI-type network without interconnection control.

Example 3.8.1 (Hardware implementation of a TBI-type network)
Consider the TBI-*type network shown in Figure 3.25. The net is built up from $N = 7$ nodes, $I = 2$ input nodes, and $O = 1$ output nodes. Thus, the number of links is given by $2(N - I) = 10$. As each link has two interfering inputs (I_A and I_B), the number of connection-control bits is $2 \cdot 2 \cdot (N - I) = 20$. Typically, the following entity* tbi_net *would have programmed:*

```
entity tbi_net is
  port (clk     : in  std_logic;
        reset   : in  std_logic;
        netin   : in  std_logic_vector (1 downto 0);
        links   : in  std_logic_vector (19 downto 0);
        netout  : out std_logic);
end tbi_net;
```

The entity has a global reset and a global clock signal. The inputs must be fed into netin, *and the interconnection switches are controlled by* links. *The single bit network output is* netout. *The detailed listing can be found on the book web-site.*

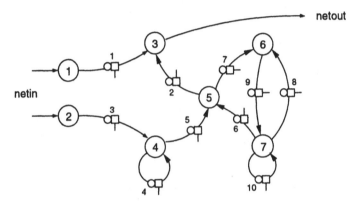

Fig. 3.25. Sample TBI-type network to be implemented in hardware.

Compiling the tbi_net *entity with Synopsys[1], a professional compiler and circuit synthesis tool, results in a high performance design. The target device was a Xilinx Virtex[2] XCV1000BG560 with a speed grade of −4. The network runs at legendary 156MHz after placement and routing with the Xilinx design manager (Alliance). The chip area used is about 24 slices. Note that a Virtex slice mainly contains two look-up tables (LUT) and two D flip-flops. One Virtex CLB is organized in two similar slices. For more details see [216]. It would be possible to put about 5,000 nodes in a Xilinx XCV1000.* ∎

The above example has shown that a TBI-type network can very efficiently be implemented in FPGAs. It is possible to run very large networks at high clock frequencies—an advantage of weightless systems! However, it is important to see that Turing networks cannot be compared with conventional

[1] Synopsys is a registered trademark of Synopsys Inc.
[2] Xilinx and Virtex are registered trademarks of Xilinx Inc.

neural networks in terms of the number of nodes only. Neurons of conventional neural networks are much more complicated—and thus also more powerful—than Turing neurons. Furthermore, an important part of the network has not yet been considered: the control of the TBI-type links! Typically, one would also need the following sub-systems that naturally depend on the learning algorithm used and on the task the network has to perform (see also Figure 3.26):

- *Connection control entity.* Reduces the number of control bits and may perform additional control task in order to simplify the learning supervisor module.
- *Pattern presentation entity.* Is responsible for presenting the patterns and determining the output pattern of the network.
- *Learning supervisor.* Orchestrates the learning process, the presentation of patterns, and the modification of the connection switches.
- *Pattern memory.* For large databases, a special (external) pattern memory might be necessary and useful.

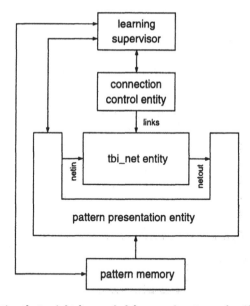

Fig. 3.26. Entities that might be needed for a real pattern classification system in hardware.

4. Organizing Unorganized Machines

Any sufficiently advanced technology is indistinguishable from magic.
— Arthur C. Clarke, *Profiles of the Future*, 1962.

The past years have produced an impressive amount of research on machine learning. Learning generally allows a system to improve its performance by experience. Historically, the earliest forms of supervised learning (learning with a teacher) involved changing the synaptic weights so as to minimize the error of the network. Today, one of the most popular learning techniques is the back-propagation algorithm: the error of the output units is propagated back into the network to yield estimates of how much a given hidden unit contributed to the global output error. The estimates are then used to adjust the synaptic weights. There are currently a large number of learning algorithms used to change the synaptic weights of many kinds of neural networks. A lot of work is also focused on the understanding of the interaction of learning and evolution in biological systems. From an engineering point of view, the combination of learning and evolution shows that significant advantages can be gained in the adaptation of systems to an environment for a given task. We shall see in this chapter an evolutionary learning approach for Turing neural networks.

In his 1947 paper, Turing rather naively suggested that the infant human cortex should be considered as an unorganized machine. This statement might certainly be questioned since it largely oversimplifies the brain. From a biological point of view, there is a good reason to consider the embryos growing cortex as an almost unorganized network because the DNA definitely has insufficient storage capacity for the complete specification (i.e., interconnections, positions, etc.) of the entire human brain. However, the brain is neither constructed at random but the construction is guided by many self-organizing principles.

As we have seen earlier in this book, Turing's unorganized machines can be classified into two different classes:

1. machines that allow interference by some agent (e.g., BI-type or TBI-type networks) and
2. machines without the possibility of interference (e.g., A-type machines).

Turing networks that allow interference could either be organized by an external agent (supervisor) or by self-modification. Networks that do not allow interference are, once an architecture is chosen and the nodes are initialized, no longer modifiable and will thus evolve deterministically towards an attractor. Training Turing's neural networks is a process where each interconnection is set by means of its interfering inputs into a state that allows the network to perform its desired task. Classical neural networks usually have weighted connections with weights having real values. In contrast, there is nothing smooth in switching Turing's interconnections in a network. The connection is either enabled or disabled—a savage all-or-nothing shift. Thus, useless neurons are simply disconnected from the rest of the network (known as *pruning*).

This chapter deals with some methods that organize unorganized machines. Turing himself already mentioned a method called "genetical" search that will be further described and applied in this chapter. Today, this method is better known under the term *genetic algorithm*. He was probably one of the first persons who had the idea to apply an evolutionary algorithm to neural networks. In the next section, I shall first give a very brief introduction to evolutionary algorithms. Evolutionary algorithms can be applied to neural networks to find an architecture, the connection weights, or the learning rules. Different encoding techniques shall also be introduced. Evolutionary algorithms will then be used for different pattern classification problems.

4.1 Evolutionary Algorithms

Evolutionary algorithms (EA) are a collection of methodologies inspired by the principles of the biological evolution. The basic concepts go back to the work of Charles Darwin [42]. It is interesting that Turing himself already mentioned "genetical" or "evolutionary" search in his 1948 paper [192, p. 23] in the context of problem solving.

Later, John Holland first introduced and substantiated the idea of *genetic algorithms* (GAs) [93]. To date, many variations and extensions of algorithms and methods inspired by the biological evolution have been proposed. One of the most recent milestones was the introduction by John Koza [106] of a method called *genetic programming* that deals with the automatic generation of computer code. For further reading of general interest, the reader is referred to Banzhaf [20], Michalewicz [120], Bäck [16], Mitchell and Forrest [127], Koza [107], Vose [205], and Fogel [60].

The term evolutionary algorithm usually encompasses a number of related methodologies such as *genetic algorithms, evolutionary strategies, evolutionary programming, genetic programming*, etc.

Mathematically speaking, evolutionary algorithms are a broad collection of optimization methods that are particularly suitable for "hard" problems where little is known about the underlying search space. In order to optimize a solution, an evolution process is simulated, in the course of which the parameters that produce an optimal solution are determined. As biological evolution does, evolutionary algorithms maintain a population of *individuals*, each one representing a possible solution for a given optimization problem. Each individual is represented by a finite string of symbols, called *genome*. The *search space*—generally too huge to be exhaustively searched—contains all possible solutions to the problem.

The functioning of a "standard" genetic algorithm can be summarized as follows (pseudo-code):

```
Randomly initialize a population of individuals (g=0)
Evaluate the population (fitness evaluation)
repeat
  Selection g(t) <- g(t-1)
  Crossover
  Mutation
  Evaluate the population
until (best or ''good'' solution found)
```

The algorithm starts with the creation of an initial population of individuals. Usually, this population is randomly generated, however, some heuristics are sometimes applied in order to reduce the search space at the beginning. All individuals are then evaluated according to a certain *fitness function*. The next step is *selection*—according to fitness, and one of many known selection strategies—of the individuals of generation $g(t-1)$ to form a new population. In order to explore the search space, new individuals, i.e., new solutions, are created by means of the *crossover* and *mutation* operators. Crossover simply exchanges—according to some strategies—parts of the parent's genomes to create a child, also called *offspring*. The goal of this operator is to create individuals that move towards the optimal solution. Mutation, on the other hand, randomly changes some symbols on the genome with a small probability. The goal of this operator is to randomly explore the search space.

Compared to local optimization methods, i.e., gradient descent, genetic algorithms have the advantage that they less often get trapped in local minima of the function to be optimized. Since a population of solutions is used, the algorithm can "move away" from local optima if the population finds better solutions in other areas. The disadvantage of genetic algorithms is that there is no guarantee that the process converges to the optimal solution.

4.2 Evolutionary Artificial Neural Networks

Today, a lot of work is focused on the understanding of the interaction of learning and evolution in biological systems. From an engineering point of view, the combination of learning and evolution shows that significant advantages can be gained in the adaptation of systems to an environment for a given task.

Evolution and learning are two forms of biological adaptation that differ in space and time. Evolution is a selective reproduction and substitution of a population of individuals. Learning, instead, is a set of modifications taking place within each single individual during its own lifetime. Often learning also refers to the modification of synaptic weights of a neuron network during its *lifetime*. Both forms of adaptation have been successfully combined in many applications and it has been shown that, although they are two distinct forms of adaptation, they strongly influence each other [133].

4.2.1 Fundamentals

Evolutionary artificial neural networks (EANN) refer to a special class of *artificial neural networks* (ANNs) in which evolution is another fundamental form of adaption in addition to learning. Evolutionary algorithms are used to perform various tasks, such as connection weight training, architecture design, learning rule adaption, input feature selection, connection weight initialization, etc. EANN can adapt as well to an environment as to changes in the environment [217]. In a broader sense, EANNs can be regarded as as a general framework for adaptive systems, i.e., systems that change their architectures and learning rules appropriately without human intervention.

Yao classified evolution in ANNs in three different levels [217]:

1. connection weights,
2. architectures, and
3. learning rules.

The evolution of connection weights is an adaptive and global approach to training, especially in the reinforcement learning and recurrent network learning paradigm where gradient-based training algorithms often experience great difficulties. The evolution of architectures enables ANNs to adapt their topologies to different tasks without human intervention and thus provides an approach to automatic ANN design, as both ANN connection weights and structures can be evolved. Finally, the evolution of learning rules can be regarded as a process of "learning to learn" in ANNs where the adaption of learning rules is achieved through evolution.

More recent approaches try to encode the type of learning used for each neuron instead of the synaptic weights on the genome. This is more biologically plausible and the final system is more robust to environmental changes.

4.2.2 Encoding Techniques

When applying GAs to neural network design, each *genome* (also called *string* or *chromosome*) generally encodes a network architecture, the network weights, or both. The encoded network architecture is known as *genotype*. In analogy with natural genetics, the actual network architecture realized by a genotype is called *phenotype*, the structure that emerges as the result of interpretation of the genotype. The central topic of this section is the *genotype-to-phenotype mapping* on which Langton expressed:

"[...] the phenotype is a nonlinear function of the genotype, and the label of that nonlinear function is *development*" [110].

Miller *et al.* [123] have classified encoding techniques into two categories:

1. *strong specification schemes*, also called *direct encoding*, or *blueprint encoding*, and
2. *weak specification schemes*, also called *indirect encoding*.

They define the mapping from genotype to phenotype in terms of the level at which the encoding takes place. A weak network specification is defined as one which only considers structural elements at the highest level, namely the organization of layers, nodes, but not individual connections. The indirect encoding scheme is used in order to reduce the length of the genotypical representation. A strong specification scheme is a low level form of encoding in which every connection is specified individually within the genotype.

Roberts and Turega [149] proposed a third, the *intermediate representation scheme*, also known as *grammar encoding scheme* [102]. This scheme makes use of fractal techniques like *L*-systems developed by Lindenmayer [112] and extended by Prusinkiewicz [144]. The process may be compared to the growth of natural objects. For more details about connectionist modeling using *L*-systems, see for example Vaario [198].

In general, the way in which the phenotype-to-genotype coding should be realized is not straightforward. In most current models, the representations of the genotypic and phenotypic forms coincide, that is, the inherited genotype directly and literally describes the phenotypical neural network. This approach encounters problems of scalability [102] because the number of bits of information necessary to encode a network increases in general exponentially with the number of neurons of the network. Note that this is not the case with Turing neural networks as the number of connections to encode is linearly dependent on the number of network neurons (see also Section 5.1).

Roberts and Turega [149] conclude that the encoding method of a network indeed influences the quality of the networks produced. On small networks, containing only a few nodes, the strong encoding scheme was found to outperform the other encoding schemes. The grammar encoding scheme appears to be relatively unaffected by the problem size.

Yao concludes in [217] that the direct encoding scheme of ANN architectures is very good at fine tuning and generating a compact architecture. The indirect encoding scheme is suitable for finding a particular type of ANN architecture quickly. As with every evolutionary algorithm, the search for an optimal solution is usually very computationally expensive. It is thus better not to employ EAs at all possible levels (architecture, weights, learning rules) of evolution.

For further reading about encoding strategies, see also Hancock [79] and Gruau [77], for the evolutionary design of artificial neural networks see for example de Garis [48], Yao and Liu [218, 219], Yao [217], Nolfi and Floreano [133, 134], and Nolfi and Parisi [135].

4.2.3 A-type Network Encoding

Only the strong specification scheme has been used to encode A-type networks. The entire network is thus encoded in the genome and constructing the phenotype from the genotype is completely deterministic. In cases where no initial node values are needed, only the two input connections for each node must be specified. Figure 4.1 shows the direct encoding used. The genome has a length of $2(N - I) = 2D$. The inputs do not have to be encoded.

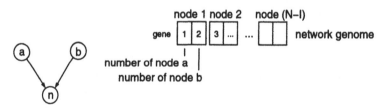

Fig. 4.1. Encoding of an A-type network genome without initial node values. The genes specify the origin (the number of the node) of the two incoming links.

As each node receives input from exactly two other nodes, the possible value for a gene is in the interval $[1...N]$. In cases where a network with initial node values needs to be evolved, the genome will have a length of $3N$ since input nodes might also get assigned an initial value. The encoding is shown in Figure 4.2. Again, each gene can have a value in the interval $[1...N]$.

Example 4.2.1 (A-type network genome encoding)
Figure 4.3 shows the resulting genome when encoding the network depicted in Figure 2.5 (Section 2.2.2). The initial values of each node are also encoded. ∎

In order to obtain a uniform genome with the same gene values in the interval $[1...N]$ all over the genome, the initial node values might be interpreted as follows when constructing the phenotype:

node 1
node 2
node N
gene
1 2 3
4 ...
...
network genome
a
b
n
v
number of node a
number of node b
value v of node 1

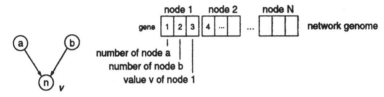

Fig. 4.2. Encoding of an A-type network genome with initial node values. The genes specify the origin (the number of the node) of the two incoming links and the initial value v.

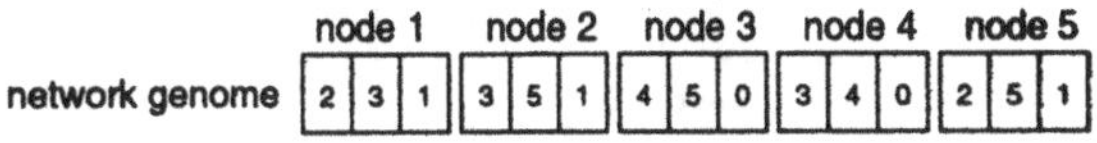

node 1
node 2
node 3
node 4
node 5
network genome
2 3 1
3 5 1
4 5 0
3 4 0
2 5 1

Fig. 4.3. A-type network genome encoding. The genome encodes the network of Figure 2.5.

$$\text{initial node value v of node i} = \begin{cases} 1 & \text{if } gene[3i] \geq \lceil N/2 \rceil \\ 0 & \text{otherwise.} \end{cases} \tag{4.1}$$

The first I input nodes specified on the genome of an A-type network are normally only required for the initial input node values. The two numbers for the incoming links are simply not interpreted and only remain there in order to obtain a uniform genome. As most networks have much fewer inputs than computing nodes, this additional and unused information is not a problem.

As one can easily see, even for a small network, the possible number of networks a genome can specify is enormous! The search space for a simple A-type network consisting of N nodes and no initial node values contains $N^{2(N-I)}$ different networks. For example, a network consisting of $I = 16$ inputs and a total of $N = 100$ nodes, the search space would contain $S_A = 100^{2(100-16)} = 100^{168} = 10^{336}$ possible networks. This is a *lot* and nobody will ever be able to test all these networks!

Note, that for most applications, a network without initial values might be used. Initial values only make sense if the A-type network has no inputs. An A-type network without inputs and without particular initial node values will be useless since all nodes will oscillate between 0 and 1 together when initialized to 0 or 1 altogether. If, for example, all nodes start at 0 (time $t = 0$), then, at time $t + 1$ (for A-type nets), all nodes will have the value 1 (remember the NAND gates!). At time $t + 2$, the node values will again all be set to 0. So no real interest here except for generating the bitstream `0,1,0,1,0,1,0,1,0,...`

4.2.4 B-type Network Encoding

The genomic encoding of B-type networks is slightly more complicated because of the interconnection switches. Figure 4.4 shows the solution adopted.
Q_1, Q_2, Q_3 are the output values of the link nodes (see Section 2.3.2).

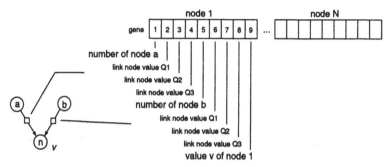

Fig. 4.4. Encoding of a B-type network genome with initial values. $Q_1 = 1, Q_2 = 0, Q_3 = 1$ refer to Section 2.3.2.

As one can easily see, the search space has become even bigger! For example, encoding a network that consists of $N = 100$ nodes requires a genome
of $100 \times 9 = 900$ genes. Assuming that each node-gene is encoded by a 7-
bit number—which is sufficient for a 100-node network since $2^7 = 128$—and
that each node value uses a 1-bit number, the genome would have a length
of $200 \times 7 + 700 = 2100$ bits! It is rather challenging to find a solution to a
given problem on a single-processor PC or workstation within a reasonable
amount of time.

A first small improvement could be achieved in the following way: in lieu
of encoding all three node values (Q_1, Q_2, Q_3) of every switch, it would be
sufficient to encode only the state of the switch, i.e., enabled or disabled.
One could then easily determine the values of Q_2, Q_3 (see also Section 2.3).
However, this simplification will only work when the metastable link states
are not being used—which is most often the case.

4.2.5 Architecture versus Configuration

In order to considerably reduce the length of the genomes, i.e., the search
space for the evolutionary algorithm, a different approach has been used for
many experiences presented in this book. First, experiments have shown that
the initial node values are of almost no importance to the performance of a
network when different input patterns are presented that have to be classified.
One can initialize them randomly or even reset them to 0 or 1 before a new
task has to be completed. Secondly, we make a difference between a *network
architecture* and a *network configuration*. A *network architecture* is defined

by a set of links interconnecting a set of nodes. Thus, the architecture does not define the state of the interconnection switches. On the other hand, the *network configuration* is defined as the set of all link switch states.

Example 4.2.2 (Network architecture)

In Example 2.5.1 we have demonstrated a two-step creation of a link state matrix. The function randllist *was thereby used to create a list of links that interconnect a set of* nnodes. *For more details see also Section 2.5.2. In the above presented terminology, the function* randllist *thus creates a network architecture.*

```
>> llist=randllist(2,8)

llist =

       1       3
       4       3
       1       4
       1       4
       4       5
       6       5
       2       6
       7       6
       5       7
       8       7
       3       8
       7       8
```

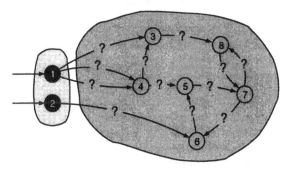

Fig. 4.5. Network architecture randomly generated by the function randllist. A network architecture defines no node values nor link states.

Figure 4.5 shows the resulting network architecture. No initial values nor link states have been specified. ■

Once a network architecture has been created, the network must be configured, i.e., the link states and the initial values must be assigned for all nodes. It is easy to see that, during configuration, no new interconnections could be created. However, links could be virtually removed by disabling them. For example, the configured network depicted in Figure 4.6 is strictly identical to the network of Figure 2.32. Nodes 3 and 8 could be removed as they have no outgoing links and are thus useless. Strictly speaking, this network is no longer a TBI-type net since there are no longer two incoming links for each node, but, as we will see later on in this book, this is not a problem but rather an advantage.

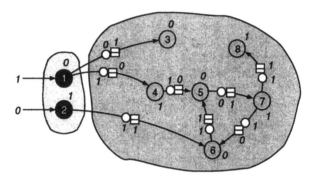

Fig. 4.6. TBI-type network that is strictly identical to the network of Figure 2.32. Disabled links have been removed. Nodes 3 and 8 are useless as they have no outgoing links.

In summary, there are at least three levels where an evolutionary process can intervene during a network construction:

1. the architectural level, i.e., the interconnections,
2. the configuration of the interconnection switches (enabled or disabled), and
3. the initialization of the node values.

Note that level two concerns the initialization of the link internal nodes 2 and 3, whereas level three concerns the initialization of the node values and of the link internal nodes 1 and inv (see also Figure 2.25). So far, all three levels were encoded on the same genome. However, experiments have shown that it is sufficient to work either on level one (the architecture) or two (the switch configuration). When working only on the architectural level, all interconnection switches are enabled (closed) and the EA tries to find a suitable architecture. On the other hand, when working on the second level, a network architecture will first be randomly generated. The EA will then only work on the switch configuration, i.e., it will open or close switches. In both cases, the initial node values are set at random. Moreover, working on the second level implies in general the use of a much larger network. This is due to the fact that no new connections can be created. The network must thus offer many more connection than needed. Otherwise, one risks being unable to fulfill a task since it is too small, i.e., some connections needed are not available. It thus often happens that larger parts of a network are completely disconnected from the rest. Disabling connections within a network is best compared with traditional neural network pruning.

Figure 4.7 shows a binary B-type genome that only encodes the interconnection switches. The architecture has been initially chosen at random. The genome length (in bits) is equal to the number of links in the network.

A two-step combination of architecture and configuration evolution could also be imagined. First, an EA tries to find a "good" architecture with all interconnections enabled. The second step consists of a sort of fine-tuning: a second EA will disable those interconnections created during the first step that are useless or even disturbing. However, what is a "good" network architecture? Experiments have shown that this is a rather difficult question that is best solved by means of some sort of heuristic. For example, consider an architecture as "good" when its fitness is better than 80%. Then continue with an adjustment of the link switches.

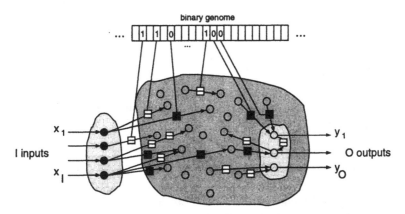

Fig. 4.7. Binary B-type network genome encoding the interconnection switches only. The genome has a length of $2(N - I)$ genes (1 = enabled, 0 = disabled).

4.2.6 L-System Encoding

L-systems, invented in 1968 by Aristid Lindenmayer [112], is a formalism that allows to efficiently describe growth, e.g., plant growth. For a particular L-system, the growth always starts from the same seed cell, called *axiom*. *Production rules* are used to describe the growth of new cells from the old cells. In this section, I am going to present an L-system with a possible interpretation that allows to represent A-type networks in a very compact way .

Example 4.2.3 (*L*-system)
Consider the L-system as shown in Table 4.1. Starting from the axiom, the rules are then simultaneously substituted as shown in Figure 4.2.

Axiom: A
Rules: A → aBab
B → aA

Table 4.1. *L*-system axiom and rules.

Depth	String
0	A
1	aBab
2	aaAab
3	aaaBabab
4	aaaaAabab
...	...

Table 4.2. Simultaneous string substitutions.

■

So far, the symbols do not have any meaning and thus, the strings by themselves, mean absolutely nothing. In the following, I will show how to construct a network architecture by means of an *L*-system. The initial node values will be initialized randomly.

Consider the following string: $S_8 = s_1 s_2 s_3 s_4 s_5 s_6 s_7 s_8 = -1\ 2\ |\ -3\ -2\ |\ 1\ -2\ |\ -5\ 0$. How do we construct a network from this string? The string contains eight symbols. Suppose we want to construct a network without input nodes. Thus, we start by drawing four network nodes that we label from 1 to 4 as shown in Figure 4.8. Then, we take node number $i = 1$ and make incoming connections from node $1 + ((i - 1 + s_1)\ mod\ 4) = 4$ and node $1 + ((i - 1 + s_2)\ mod\ 4) = 3$. The resulting network is shown in Figure 4.9. For node number $i = 2$, connections are made from node $1 + ((i - 1 + s_3)\ mod\ 4) = 3$ and node $1 + ((i - 1 + s_4)\ mod\ 4) = 4$. The mindful reader has now certainly realized that the string-symbols are interpreted as relative node-offsets. Thus, the entire network can be easily constructed. It is shown in Figure 4.10.

Fig. 4.8. Start with four network nodes numbered from 1 to 4.

Fig. 4.9. Network after the interpretation of the first two string-symbols that represent relative node-offsets.

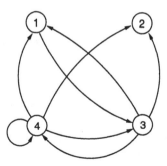

Fig. 4.10. The final network drawn from string −1 2 | −3 −2 | 1 −2 | −5 0.

Example 4.2.4 (*L*-system that encodes an A-type network)

Consider the L-system as shown in Table 4.3.

Axiom:	−2 1
Rules:	1 → 2 −3 1
	2 → −1 0 3

Table 4.3. *L*-system axiom and rules for an A-type network construction.

Starting from the axiom, the rules are simultaneously substituted as shown in Table 4.4. The network that arises when the final string of Table 4.4 is interpreted is shown in Figure 4.11.

Depth	String
0	$-2\ 1$
1	$-2\ 2\mid -3\ 1$
2	$-2\ -1\mid 0\ 3\mid -3\ 2\mid -3\ 1$

Table 4.4. A-type network string substitutions.

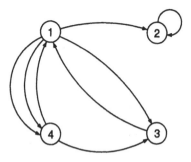

Fig. 4.11. The final network drawn from string $-2\ -1\mid 0\ 3\mid -3\ 2\mid -3\ 1$.

It is easy to see that the representation is redundant. Assume that node 2 of Figure 4.11 is being connected. The incoming connection from node 1 can be made by an offset of -1 or by 3. The advantage of an L-system and its application to Turing networks lies after all in the compactness of the representation. Starting from a simple axiom and one or several rules, very complex networks can be constructed. Thus, the substitutions of Table 4.4 could be carried on as long as desired. Compared to the previously presented network encodings (see Sections 4.2.3 and 4.2.4) where the network size was directly proportional to the size of the genome, the L-system representation is independent of the final network size. An evolutionary algorithm might be easily applied to the axiom, the rule(s), or to both. Thereby, the string symbols used depend on the maximal network size. Assume a network built up from N nodes. The string symbols should thus be chosen within the interval $[-N, N]$. If the interval is smaller, it would not be possible to reach all nodes from any other node.

4.3 Example: Evolve Networks that Regenerate Bitstreams

In the following, a rather simple experiment will be presented. The goal is to illustrate the application of genetic algorithms to Turing neural networks.

Example 4.3.1 (Binary bitstream generation)
How many neurons are required for an A-type or a B-type network so as to regenerate a binary bitstream of finite length?

A set of 22 randomly generated binary bitstreams ranging from a length of five to 25 bits has been generated by a simple C program. The bitstreams are shown in Table 4.5.

length	bitstream start...end
5	0,1,1,1,0
6	0,1,1,1,0,1
7	1,1,1,0,0,1,0
8	1,0,0,1,1,0,0,0
9	0,0,1,0,1,1,0,1,0
10	0,1,1,0,0,1,0,1,0,0
11	0,1,1,0,1,0,0,1,1,1,0
12	1,0,0,1,0,0,1,1,0,0,0,1
13	1,0,0,1,1,1,1,0,1,0,1,0,1
14	0,1,0,0,1,1,1,0,0,0,1,0,1,0
15	1,0,1,0,0,1,0,1,0,1,0,0,1,1,0
16	1,0,0,0,0,1,0,1,0,1,0,0,1,0,1,0
17	0,0,1,1,0,0,0,1,0,1,0,1,0,0,1,1,1
18	1,0,0,1,1,0,0,0,1,1,0,0,1,0,1,0,1,0
19	0,0,0,1,0,1,1,0,1,0,1,1,1,0,1,0,0,1,0
20	0,1,1,0,1,0,1,0,0,0,1,0,1,1,1,0,0,1,1,0
21	1,0,0,1,0,0,1,0,0,0,1,0,0,0,1,0,1,0,1,0,1
22	0,0,1,0,1,1,0,0,0,0,1,0,1,0,1,0,0,1,1,1,0,0
23	0,0,1,1,0,1,0,1,1,0,1,0,1,0,1,0,0,0,1,0,1,0,1
24	1,0,0,1,0,1,0,1,0,0,1,0,0,0,1,0,1,0,0,1,0,1,0,1
25	1,0,1,0,1,0,0,1,0,1,0,0,1,0,1,1,1,0,1,0,1,0,1,0,0

Table 4.5. Randomly generated finite binary bitstreams used for regeneration by A-type and B-type networks.

The goal of the A-type and B-type networks was then to correctly regenerate the bitstreams using a minimum of network nodes. Thereby, a different network has been used for every bitstream. The network architecture used is depicted in Figure 4.12. It only has one output node—the output for the bitstream—and no input nodes. The genetic algorithm also had to find the correct initial values of each node. For both A-type and B-type networks, the encoding (with initial values) as shown in Figure 4.2 and Figure 4.4 has been used.

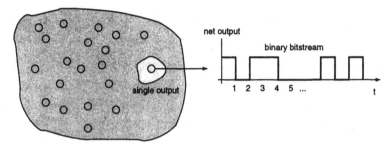

Fig. 4.12. Architecture of the machines used for regenerating binary bitstreams of five to 25 bits.

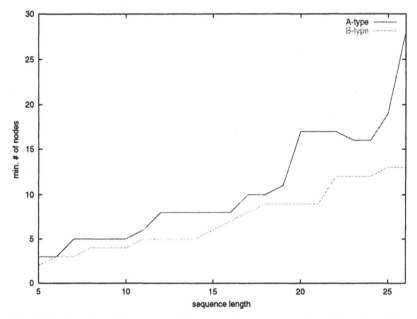

Fig. 4.13. Results of the random bitstream regeneration. They show the minimal number of necessary network nodes in function of the bitstream length. The fitness is defined as the number of correctly regenerated bits.

For each bitstream, the genetic algorithm first started trying to regenerate the bits by a 1-node network. When unsuccessful, the network size was increased by one node. This process was repeated until a network was found that regenerated the bitstream. Figure 4.13 and Table 4.6 show the results obtained. The fitness was simply defined as the number of correctly generated bits, i.e., if the reference bitstream is 0,1,1,0,1,0,0,1,1,1,0 and the bitstream generated by the network is 0,1,1,1,0,0,1,1,1,0,0, then the fitness is seven because seven out of the 11 bits are correctly regenerated:

```
reference bitstream:      r = 01101001110
regenerated bitstream:    g = 01110011100
                              |||  | || |
correctly regenerated bits:  111  1 11 1 = 7.
```

*The highest possible fitness-value is thus equal to the length of the
bitstream to generate. The genetic algorithm worked with the steady-state
selection algorithm and with a population of 100 individuals. After 30,000
generations, evolution was stopped and the network size increased.*

Bitstream length	A-type nodes	B-type nodes
5	3	2
6	3	3
7	5	3
8	5	4
9	5	4
10	5	4
11	6	5
12	8	5
13	8	5
14	8	5
15	8	6
16	8	7
17	10	8
18	10	9
19	11	9
20	17	9
21	17	9
22	17	12
23	16	12
24	16	12
25	19	13

Table 4.6. Results of the random bitstream regeneration. The second and last
column show the number of network nodes necessary so as to regenerate a bitstream
of given length.

*As one can see, a B-type machine needs fewer neurons than an A-type
machine to regenerate the same bitstream. This is not especially astonishing since a B-type machine is composed of $N + 6(N - I)$ simple neurons,
whereas an A-type machine only has N neurons. Thus, a B-type network
is computationally more powerful—at least for this toy application—than
an A-type network with the same number of neurons. The results also show
that fewer neurons than the length of the bitstream are necessary.*

*The reader has to be aware that results might be different with a differ-
ent GA and with different parameters. There is no guarantee that the solutions found are optimal, as the following example will show. Figure 4.14
shows the A-type network obtained that regenerates the 18-bit bitstream.*

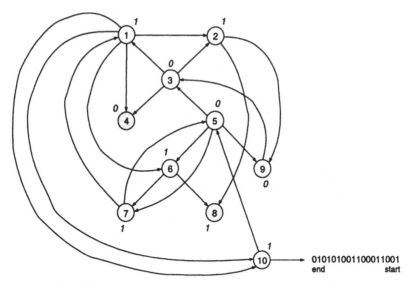

Fig. 4.14. Evolved A-type network that regenerates the 18-bit bitstream.

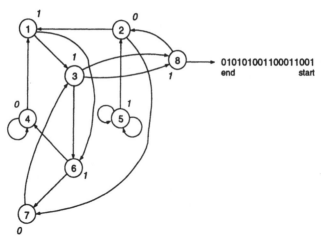

Fig. 4.15. New A-type network without useless nodes that correctly regenerates the 18-bit bitstream.

Values in italics represent initial values. As one can see, nodes 4 and 8 are useless as they have no outputs. The bitstream could be regenerated with less than ten nodes. Another experiment was performed. This time, the GA had a maximum of 100,000 generations to find a solution before the network size was increased. Figure 4.15 shows the new machine, and this time no useless nodes are present. For illustrative purposes, Figure 4.16

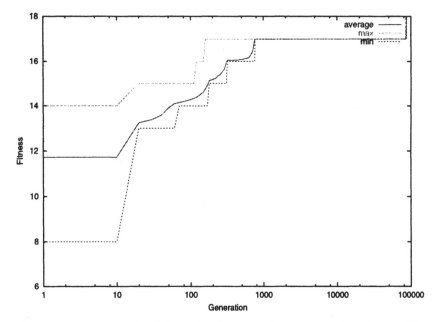

Fig. 4.16. Fitness graph of the 18-bit bitstream A-type network evolution. The bitstream is correctly regenerated at generation $84,960$.

shows the fitness graph obtained during evolution. Note, that the present solution has been found almost at the end (i.e., at generation 84,960)

∎

4.4 Signal Processing in Turing Networks

How will information in Turing networks be interpreted and processed? How are input and output patterns (vectors) presented and interpreted? How is time interpreted? How do we deal with the inherent network latency due to the D flip-flops? These questions have to be addressed as soon as one starts working with temporal patterns and Turing neural networks.

Today, many different methods, representations, etc., for signal processing in neural networks exist. Almost all methods are very application specific. What is good for one application is often less interesting for other applications. As Turing's networks are built up from very simple neurons, we are looking for a signal processing method that is simple and does not require additional units more complicated than the network itself. Furthermore, it would be of a great interest to build up eventual additional units from all and the same network nodes.

Time underlies many interesting human behaviours and is clearly important in cognition. Temporal pattern processing is widely used in hearing, speech, and vision. Because we live in an ever-changing environment, an intelligent system (human or machine), must be able to encode patterns over time, and recognize and produce temporal patterns [209]. Temporal pattern processing is a rather challenging topic as the information needed is embodied in time and thus inherently dynamic and not simultaneously available. Fundamentally different from static pattern processing, temporal processing requires a neural network having a capacity of *short-term memory (STM)* in order to maintain a component for some time. This capacity is necessary because a temporal pattern stretches over a certain time period.

The question of how to represent time has been asked by Elman [53]. As an obvious way of dealing with patterns having a temporal extent, he proposed to represent time explicitly by associating the serial order of the patterns with the dimensionality of the pattern vector. The first temporal event is represented by the first element in the pattern vector, the second by the second element, and so on. The entire pattern is then processed by the model. This proposal has several drawbacks. First, it requires some interface (shift-register) with the world that buffers the inputs. The second point is a logic problem: how should a system know when a buffer's contents should be examined? Then, a shift-register at the input imposes a rigid limit on the duration of patterns and also suggests that all input vectors are of the same length. However, the most serious problem is that this approach does not easily distinguish relative temporal position from absolute temporal position.

Another different possibility is allowing time to be represented by the effect it has on processing. This means giving the processing system dynamic properties that are responsive to temporal sequences [53], in other words, the network must be given memory, which is exactly the case for all Turing neural networks.

For Hugo de Garis' famous CAM-brain machine, Korkin et al. [105] propose the *Spike Interval Information Coding (SIIC)* representation. The SIIC representation—a sequence of bits or spikes—is inspired by Rieke et al. [148]. The procedure for decoding such a spike train consists of convolving it with a special *convolution filter*. The result obtained is called the *estimated signal*, a time-dependent signal that is output from the neural network module. The inverse process, namely, an algorithm which takes as input a binary numbered time-dependent ("analog") signal and outputs a spike train, uses a *deconvolution filter*. The SIIC representation is rather complicated and requires additional convolution and deconvolution filters.

Another interesting coding is *stochastic bitstream coding*. The central idea is to represent a real-valued signal using stochastic binary sequences. A real value $v \in [-1, 1]$ is represented using a stochastic sequence in which the probability of each bit being set to one is $\frac{v+1}{2}$ [200]. Given two independent bit

sequences of this type, the product of the two bitstreams is simply obtained
by calculating the exclusive-or (XOR) of the two bitstreams.

One of the drawbacks of stochastic bitstream coding is that each bitstream
has to be generated independently. For N bitstreams, N non-correlated random generators are required. In general, this coding method is only interesting if the entire neural network architecture has been designed for (see for
example Daalen et al. [200]).

For Turing neural networks, a different approach has been chosen. It is
easy to see that for each architecture, a Turing network has a different latency.
There is no general rule that allows to determine the exact time a signal, once
presented on the inputs, needs to traverse the network. In reality, as soon as
the inputs change, the outputs start changing very quickly too. Even for
large networks, the outputs often change after one clock cycle. When the
inputs remain unchanged for some time, the outputs start to settle down,
i.e., the network "falls" in an attractor (see also Section 5.7). This property
will be used to interpret the network's outputs. Figure 4.17 shows a typical
network output activity. The network output activity will be further defined
and presented in Section 5.8. So far, you only have to know that it is a
measure for the number of changes the output nodes make over a certain
period of time. Frequently changing nodes have high activities, stable nodes
have low activities. The figure shows that the output nodes frequently change
their values at the beginning of the pattern presentation cycle, then, the
outputs become more and more stable. This example has been ran for $T = 50$
clock cycles (steps)—which is rather a lot. Experiments have shown that even
for large networks (up to 10,000 neurons), about ten to 20 clock cycles are
enough to stabilize the outputs sufficiently. In addition, the method we use to
determine the output pattern is tolerant to a certain level of output astability.
It should, however, also be mentioned that there exist networks that do not
become stable. An example is shown in Figure 4.18. The network is trapped
in a limited state cycle and the activity thus has a periodic behaviour.

Let us run a network with five outputs for five clock cycles. At its inputs,
a certain pattern has been presented for the same time. Suppose that this
network produced the output vectors as shown in Table 4.7.

Network output	t	$t+1$	$t+2$	$t+3$	$t+4$	Resulting pattern
y_1	1	0	1	0	1	1
y_2	0	1	0	0	0	0
y_3	1	1	1	1	0	1
y_4	1	0	0	1	1	1

Table 4.7. Output vectors of a network and resulting output pattern calculated
by Equation 4.2.

The resulting output pattern is obtained by Equation 4.2. In other words,
the resulting output element y_i is set to 1 if, during the T steps, more 1s than

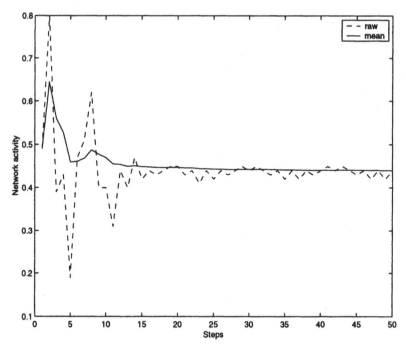

Fig. 4.17. Typical network activity of a 100-node TBl-type network during one pattern presentation cycle. The output nodes rapidly settle down and become stable.

0s were present at the output, otherwise, it will be set to 0. This method is not a real *nearest-neighbour* method since no distance between vectors is calculated.

$$y_i = \begin{cases} 1 & \text{if } \sum_{t=1}^{T} y_i[t] > T/2 \\ 0 & \text{otherwise.} \end{cases} \tag{4.2}$$

The process of classifying a pattern by means of a Turing network can be summarized as shown in algorithm 1, below.

This can all easily be done in software, however, what about a hardware implementation? Figure 4.19 shows a schematical block diagram of a possible implementation. Each network output is fed into a processing unit that stores the output values during T clock cycles and then calculates the resulting pattern. Two counters—one for the 1s and another for the 0s—and a comparator to deliver the final result would do it. Without too much difficulties, it would even be possible to implement these units using Turing nodes only.

In summary, the proposed solution for working with static patterns requires the presence of the pattern on the network inputs for several clock

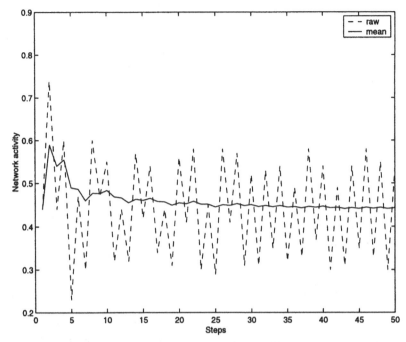

Fig. 4.18. Network activity of a 100-node TBI-type network that does not settle down, i.e., that is trapped in a limited state cycle.

Algorithm 1 Classification of one pattern with a Turing network

---

Reset the network nodes to 0 or 1. This guarantees the same initial conditions for all classifications.

Present the pattern at the network inputs.

for $t = 1$ to E time steps **do**

  Run network.

end for

Determine the network output (classification) with Equation 4.2.

Remove pattern from the inputs.

---

cycles, and thus, no continuous bitstream can be used. The network output is interpreted in a "fuzzy" way that allows dealing with unstable outputs. The method is simple and easy to implement. In this book, all pattern inputs were supposed to be available in parallel and no continuous bitstream has been used.

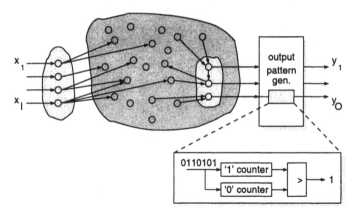

Fig. 4.19. Schematic diagram of an output pattern generator implementation in hardware.

4.5 Pattern Classification

Much of the research effort on neural networks has focused on pattern classification. *Pattern recognition* or *pattern classification* is the problem of classifying objects, often represented as vectors or as strings of symbols, into categories. Because most pattern recognition problems are too complex to be solved entirely by handcrafted algorithms, machine learning has always played a central role in pattern recognition. The difficulty is to synthesize, and then to efficiently compute, the classification function that maps objects to categories, given that objects in a category can have widely varying input representations. In most instances, the task is known to the designer through a set of example patterns whose categories are known. Important application areas are image analysis, character recognition, speech analysis, man and machine diagnostics, person identification and industrial inspection.

In the remainder of this section I shall briefly describe some exemplary and historic approaches to pattern classification. I recommend Duda et al. [52] for further reading.

One of the earliest attempts to classify patterns by machine came from Olivier Selfridge [160, 161] in 1958. Courageously, he stated: "Can a machine think? The answer is certainly: yes". Selfridge contributed a significant model called *Pandemonium* for parallel processing, a model that was able to learn to classify patterns.

> "A pattern-recognition system must learn. But how much? [...] The initial state of such a system is called a 'random net'. A large number of on-off computer elements are multiply interconnected in a random way. [...] The threshold of the elements (the number of signals that must be received before the element fires) are then adjusted on the basis of performance. In other words, the system learns by

reinforcing some pathways through the net and weakening others. How far a random net can evolve is controversial" [161].

The Pandemonium was developed with the hope of learning to recognize patterns that have not been specified. The example used was that of translating from manually keyed Morse code to a written message. Selfridge first presented an idealized Pandemonium [160] that he extended to an amended model as shown in Figure 4.20 . The *data demons* at the bottom serve to store and pass on the data. The *computation demons*, also called *subdemons*, perform certain more or less complicated computations. On the next level, the *cognitive demons* weight the "evidence": "Each cognitive demon computes a shriek, and from all the shrieks the highest level demon of all, the *decision demon*, merely selects the loudest". By means of several adaptive changes in the system (feature weighting, subdemon selection, etc.), the Pandemonium was able to "learn". The creation of new subdemons is of particular interest since a sort evolutionary method is used. Given two "useful" subdemons, a new demon is created by combining their two functions.

"The scheme sketched is really a sort of natural selection on the processing demons. If they serve a useful function they will survive, and perhaps even the source of other subdemons who are themselves judged on their merits" [160].

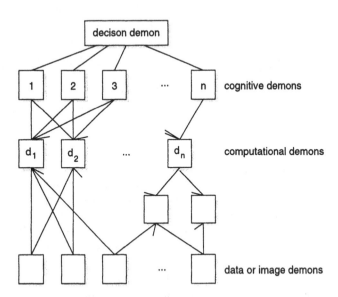

Fig. 4.20. Selfridge's amended Pandemonium.

Despite many critical voices, two years later, the Pandemonium system was able to identify ten hand-printed characters, and was tested on samples of

A, E, I, L, M, N, O, R, S, and T [161]. Six levels were used for the recognition process:

1. input,
2. clean-up,
3. inspection of features,
4. comparison with learned feature distribution,
5. computation of probabilities, and
6. the decision.

The input was given in the form of a 32×32-cell matrix.

At almost the same time, Rosenblatt [152] proposed his *perceptron*, a more general computational model than the McCulloch-Pitts units. The essential innovation was the introduction of numerical weights and special interconnection patterns. In the original Rosenblatt model the computing units are threshold elements and the connectivity is determined stochastically. Learning takes place by adapting the weights of the network with a numerical algorithm. Rosenblatt's model was refined and perfected in the 1960's and its computational properties were carefully analyzed by Minsky and Papert [125]. The classical perceptron is in fact a whole network for the solution of certain pattern recognition problems [150]. Single perceptrons can be thought of as *feature detectors*. They compute the similarity of the pattern to the ideal pattern they have been designed to identify, and the threshold is the minimal similarity that we require from the pattern. The problem with this pattern recognition scheme is that it only works if the patterns have been normalized in some way, that is, if they have been centred in the window to which the perceptron connects and their size does not differ appreciably from the ideal pattern. An alternative way of handling this problem is to try to detect patterns not in a single step, but in several stages.

In 1971, Amari [9] published a paper about learning patterns and pattern sequences by self-organizing nets of threshold elements with the intention of understanding some aspects of information processing in nervous systems. He showed that two statistical parameters are sufficient to determine the characteristics of networks.

The *cognitron* and *neocognitron* were designed by Fukushima [64,65] as an attempt to deal with the above problems and in some way to try to mimic the structure of the human vision pathway. The main idea of the neocognitron is to transform the contents of the screen into other screens in which some features have been enhanced, and again into other screens, and so on until a final decision is made. This structure is known in the image processing community as a pyramidal architecture in which the resolution is reduced by a factor of four from plane to plane. An application of the neocognitron to handwritten character recognition can be found in [66].

Character recognition is a typical field of application for automatic classification methods. In addition to its practical interest (zip code recognition, automatic reading, etc.) it exhibits all the typical problems encountered when dealing with classification: choice of the data representation, choice of a classifier of suitable type and structure, and supervised training of the classifier using a set of examples.

Next, different "toy" character and pattern recognition experiments performed with Turing networks shall be presented, mainly for illustrative purposes. Since this work is of rather historical interest, I was neither keen to enter into competition with today's well-known and certainly better performing recognition techniques, nor to directly compare the performance of the Turing networks with other classes of neural networks.

4.6 Examples: Pattern Classification with Genetic Algorithms

As already seen in Section 4.1, any genetic algorithm works with a population of individuals that mate and underlay mutation. In our case, the genome encodes either a network architecture, a network configuration, or both. In order to select the best individuals in a population, each individual is evaluated and is assigned a fitness value.

In the following examples, a very simple pattern classifier system based on Turing's networks will be used (Figure 4.21). Classically, the recognition process is divided into several *preprocessing* steps and subsequent classification. Preprocessing has not been considered and all patterns are supposed to be centred and correctly scaled. The raw data is thus directly used as a feature vector.

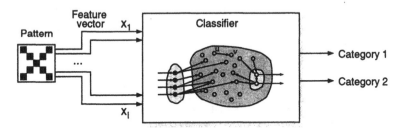

Fig. 4.21. Simple pattern classifier system used with Turing networks.

Algorithm 2 shows how to present a set of patterns to a network (i.e., an individual in a population) and how to calculate the fitness of one individual. Each pattern in the set will be individually presented to the network after all network nodes have been set to 0 (or 1). The network will then be run for E steps so as to determine the output pattern, i.e., the category the current pattern is assigned to. As the network is set to an initial state before a new pattern is presented, the order of the pattern presentation is unimportant.

For each pattern, the *Hamming* distance (see Definition 4.6.1) between the actual ($\overrightarrow{y}$) and the desired ($\overrightarrow{dp}$) output vector is calculated.

Algorithm 2 Fitness evaluation of one individual in the population (one network)

Reset the network nodes to 0 or 1. This guarantees the same initial conditions for all classifications.
for all patterns p **do**
    Present pattern p_i at the network inputs.
    for $t = 1$ to E time steps **do**
        Run network.
    end for
    Determine the network output (classification) with Equation 4.2.
    Remove pattern from the inputs.
end for
Calculate network fitness with Equation 4.6.2.

Definition 4.6.1 (Hamming distance)
The Hamming distance $d(\overrightarrow{x}, \overrightarrow{y})$ between $\overrightarrow{x}$ and $\overrightarrow{y}$ is the number of places in which $\overrightarrow{x}$ and $\overrightarrow{y}$ differ [214]. ∎

The actual network output ($\overrightarrow{y}$) is then calculated by means of Equation 4.2. Suppose now that P patterns, each output category coded by O bits (i.e., the number of network outputs), are present in the pattern database. Thus, the fitness of the network is defined as follows:

Definition 4.6.2 (Fitness of a network)

$$f = \sum_{p=1}^{P}(O - d(\overrightarrow{y}, \overrightarrow{dp})) \tag{4.3}$$

Where P is the number of patterns in the pattern database and $O = |\overrightarrow{y}|$ the number of outputs the network has (output vector length). ∎

Thus, the higher the fitness, the better the network performs its classification task. It can easily be seen that the highest possible fitness of a network, i.e., the network correctly classifying each pattern, is given, as a consequence of Equation 4.6.2, by $\sum_{p=1}^{P} O = PO$.

The fitness is evaluated for each network in the current GA-population and the selection algorithm—in all the examples presented below, the steady-state selection algorithm has been used—selects the individual networks according to their fitness value.

In the following examples, mainly A-type or BS-type networks are used. As explained earlier (see Section 2.4.4), BS-type networks need fewer resources and the signal propagation is faster (there are no D flip-flops in the links) compared to TBI-type networks. Simulation is thus much faster and larger networks might be simulated.

Let us start first with a rather simple pattern classification problem.

Example 4.6.1 (5 × 5 dot pattern classification)
The goal of this example is to classify simple two-class patterns using an A-type network. Figure 4.22 and Figure 4.23 show the ox-patterns that were designed by hand. Each pattern is defined within a 5 × 5 dot matrix, well centred and scaled. Thus, the classifier network must have 5 × 5 = 25 inputs and two outputs as there are two classes of patterns (o and x) to be classified. A network with 80 neurons has been used to classify the 20 patterns. Table 4.8 summaries the parameters used for the network and the genetic algorithm. mEvolSteps indicates the number of clock cycles the network has run so as to determine the output pattern. This parameter corresponds to parameter T described in Section 4.4, Equation 4.2. The fitness that directly indicates the number of correctly classified patterns during evolution is plotted in Figure 4.24. The network successfully learned to classify all patterns after about 4,000 generations. Note, that for this experiment, the patterns were separated in a learning and a validation set. However, the network does not show any sign of overfitting, as often happens. There are not enough patterns to be separated into two subsets.

Fig. 4.22. 5 × 5 dot ox training patterns.

Fig. 4.23. 5 × 5 dot ox validation patterns.

The same classification has been done with BS-type networks. This time, the network architecture was randomly generated and the genetic algorithm only controlled the switches (i.e., enabled or disabled). The network was built up from 500 nodes and was much bigger than the previously

Parameter	Value
Input nodes	25
Output nodes	2
Network nodes	80
Popsize	50
maxGenerations	30,000
pMutation	0.25
pCrossover	1
pReplacement	0.25
mEvolSteps	15

Table 4.8. A-type network and GA parameters.

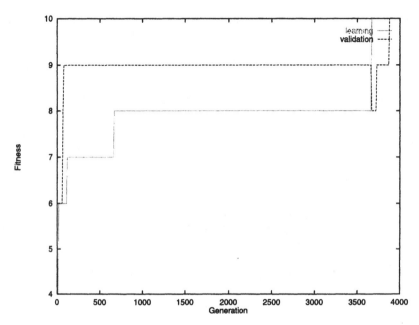

Fig. 4.24. Evolution of the network fitness during the recognition of twenty 5 × 5 dot patterns by an A-type network. The graph shows the average fitness of the training and the validation set.

used A-type network. The population size was increased to 100 *individuals, which also increased considerably the computational power required for the simulation. As Figure 4.25 shows, the network was able to classify* 19 *out of* 20 *patterns after* 10,000 *generations.*

∎

Example 4.6.2 (16 × 16 dot pattern classification)

A harder experiment consists in classifying without preprocessing twenty 16 × 16 *dot patterns into their two associated classes (x and o). The patterns are shown in Figure 4.26. An A-type network was able to classify*

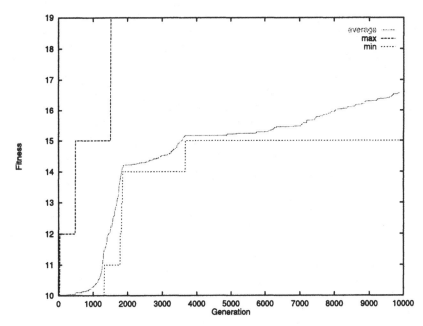

Fig. 4.25. Evolution of the network fitness during the recognition of twenty 5 × 5 dot patterns by an BS-type network with random initial architecture. The GA controls the interconnection switches only.

all patterns without to much difficulty (see Figure 4.27). The network was built up by $N = 1,000$ nodes, $I = 256$ inputs, and $O = 2$ outputs. The population size was set to 100 individuals.

On the other hand, a BS-type network was also successful (see Figure 4.28). However, during the first 200 generations, the network architecture has only been evolved. Thereby, all switches were enabled. After 200 generations, the interconnections found were "frozen" and a new genetic algorithm adjusted the switches only. Again, the network was built up from $N = 100$ nodes.

∎

Example 4.6.3 (The "Nine" patterns)

Rueckl et al. [155] proposed nine different 3 × 3 dot patterns placed on a 5 × 5 grid (see Figure 4.29). Thus, besides recognizing the form of the patterns, the network should also encode the place of the patterns on the larger input grid. Rueckl et al. conducted these experiments in an attempt to explain why in the natural visual system "what" and "where" are processed by separate cortical structures. They trained a number of different networks with 25 input nodes, 18 output nodes, and one hidden layer with 18 nodes. The 18 output nodes were separated in two groups: one for encoding the form and another for encoding the place.

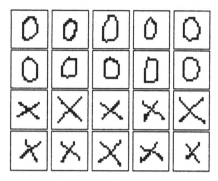

Fig. 4.26. 16 × 16 dot OX patterns.

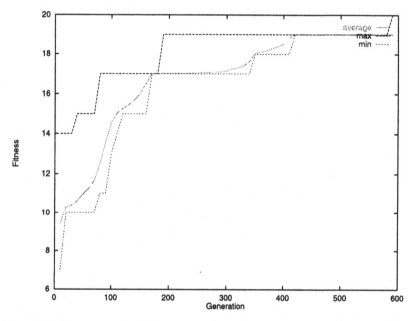

Fig. 4.27. Fitness graph of the 16 × 16 dot pattern classification by an 100-node A-type network.

The task was simplified slightly and the Turing network had to classify the patterns in a simple 3 × 3 grid only. An A-type network with 20 nodes, nine inputs, and four outputs that encoded the nine possible patterns was not really successful: the best solution found was able to classify seven out of nine patterns. Boers et al. [23] found a very simple network without hidden layer.

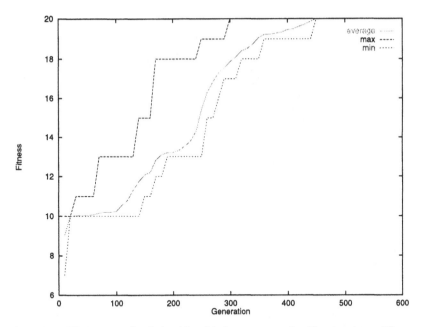

Fig. 4.28. Fitness graph of the 16 × 16 dot pattern classification by a BS-type network. A network architecture has been evolved during the first 200 generations (all switches were enabled), then only the interconnection switches were modified.

Fig. 4.29. The "Nine" patterns.

Example 4.6.4 (The "TC" problem)

The TC patterns are a set of 3 × 3 dot letters T and C, rotated by 0, 90, 180, or 270 degrees within a grid of 4 × 4 dots [156]. Furthermore, the letters can be placed anywhere on the grid. Figure 4.30 shows that there are 32 possible patterns. Boers et al. [23] found a network to this problem with 13 input nodes only.

It turned out that the TC problem is rather difficult to solve for Turing neural networks. A combined evolution on the architecture and the network configuration was used. A 100-node BS-type network successfully classified only 19 out of 32 patterns.

∎

Example 4.6.5 (Classification with a feed-forward network)

So far, the networks could freely interconnect, at the exception of the two inputs for each network node. The resulting networks were thus always highly recurrent and without any organization in form of layers—which

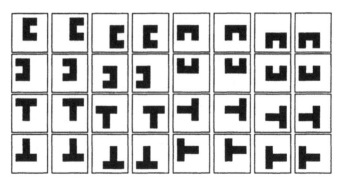

Fig. 4.30. The TC patterns.

exactly meets the ideas of Turing. I was just curious to see how a randomly interconnected feed-forward network would behave and thus performed some tests.

The networks used in the present experiment were only allowed to make connections in the forward direction. Figure 4.31 shows an example of a feed-forward A-type Turing network. It turned out—which was not really a surprise—that the feed-forward network architecture offers less performance than a recurrent architecture, at least for the pattern recognition tasks performed. The reason is probably that the network does not have an internal memory when organized in a feed-forward manner. The fitness graph of a typical 5 × 5 dot ox-pattern classification is depicted in Figure 4.32. It shows that only 16 out of 20 patterns were correctly classified after 100,000 generations. The network was built from 200 nodes.

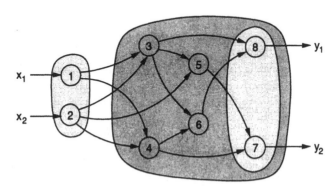

Fig. 4.31. Feed-forward A-type network architecture. There are no recurrent connections allowed and the network thus has no internal state.

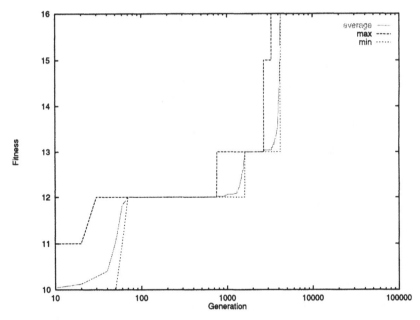

Fig. 4.32. 5 × 5 dot ox-pattern classification with a 200-node A-type feed-forward network. Only 16 out of 20 patterns were correctly classified.

4.7 A Learning Algorithm for Turing Networks

Turing's viewpoint of machine intelligence and machine "education" was always rather optimistic and he believed—or at least saw no reason not to believe—that there would turn out to be no essential difference between what could be achieved by a human intellect and what could be achieved by a machine [71]. Today, one would perhaps be more careful with similar assertions since it seems that we are still far away from any machine with human-like intelligence, although some people would not share this opinion (e.g., R. Kurzweil [109]).

Turing's basic ideas were as follows:

> "In the process of trying to imitate an adult human mind we are bound to think a good deal about the process which has brought it to the state that it is in. We may notice three components, (a) The initial state of the mind, say at birth, (b) The education to which it has been subjected, (c) Other experience, not to be described as education, to which it has been subjected. Instead of trying to produce a program to simulate the adult mind, why not rather try to produce one which simulates the child's? If this were then subjected to an appropriate course of education one would obtain the adult brain" [188, p. 455] [194].

Turing thus divided the process of "education" into two parts: (1) the child's program and (2) the educational process. This separation can still be used today: the child's program corresponds to the initial network architecture and to the initial values whereas the educational process corresponds to some learning algorithm that modifies ("trains") the network. However, Turing never really went into details and his learning procedures remained vague.

Today, a big deal of neural network learning algorithms is known that has been successfully applied to many problems (see for example Haykin [84]). Classical neural networks usually have weighted connections with weights having real values. In contrast, there is nothing smooth in switching introverted pairs of a Turing network. The connection is either enabled or disabled—a savage all-or-nothing shift. The drawback of an all-or-nothing shift is that a training algorithm cannot continuously increment and decrement the connection weights in order to improve the network overall performance. On the other hand, it is much easier to control binary-valued connections than real-valued ones and the number of possible network configurations is considerably reduced.

Boolean networks can learn and generalize from what has been learned. A rather dramatic example has for example been presented by Patarnello and Carnevali [139]: A boolean network with 160 neurons (gates) was trained to correctly add randomly chosen pairs of 8-bit numbers. The network was then able to give the correct result for all the remaining pairs (the total number of pairs being 2^{16}!). In [28, 140] they conclude that learning takes place as a phase transition and that problems with high *entropy*—a high number of network configurations—are easy to learn.

Patarnello and Carnevali used *simulated annealing* [108]—a powerful optimization tool based on statistical mechanics methods—to optimize their networks. Simulated annealing is often used to optimize the behaviour of complex systems of many parameters and it was mainly introduced for the automatic design of VLSI circuits (very large scale integration).

Patarnello and Carnevali's networks were made up of N_G gates, each gate having two inputs (remember Turing's networks!) and an arbitrary number of outputs. The gate realizes one of 16 possible boolean functions with two variables. In their experiments, they only used feed-forward networks. Each node could receive input from either the input bits or from one of the preceding gates.

The main difference between their work and other work is that they:

> "[...] look at the problem as a *global* optimization problem, without assigning *ad hoc* rules to back-propagate corrections on some nodes" [139].

The optimization is performed as a Monte Carlo procedure towards zero temperature. The system's energy function E is the difference between the correct result and the one obtained from the circuit, averaged over the number of examples presented to the system. An optimization step consists in changing an input connection of a gate, the calculation of the resulting energy change, and the acceptance of the change with a certain probability.

Inspired by Patarnello and Carnevali's approach, the following algorithm is proposed for Turing's TBI-type networks:

Algorithm 3 Simulated annealing for TBI-type networks

Choose a randomly connected network architecture ($K = 2$).
Choose a random switch configuration.
Randomly initialize the network nodes.
repeat
  Change a connection switch at random.
  Calculate the resulting energy change ΔE (difference between the correct result and the desired result).
  Accept the changing with probability $e^{-\frac{\Delta E}{T}}$ (Boltzman factor), where T is the temperature that slowly decreases towards zero according to some annealing schedule.
until done

The problem with simulated annealing is that it tends to get stuck at a local maximum and never reaches the global maximum. The temperature T introduces noise in the system and allows the system to "jump" out of local maxima. Another tactic is to apply some heuristics or to start from different initial conditions. So far, the development of annealing schedules that work with a large class of different problems is a challenge yet to be met.

Broeck and Kawai [49] also used simulated annealing to train their feedforward boolean networks (the model was the same as Carnevali and Patarnello's). Their detailed analysis has shown that the probability distribution for the number of boolean functions scales as an inverse power law of their probability. This law is commonly known as *Zipf's law* [221] and indicates the existence of an underlying *fractal structure*.

5. Network Properties and Characteristics

The aim of science is not to open the door to infinite wisdom,
but to set a limit to infinite error.
— Berthold Brecht, *The Life of Galileo*, 1939.

Biological neural networks are extremely rich in complexity and dynamics. Nobel Laureate John Eccles once described the human brain as the most complex system in the universe. The investigation of artificial and natural neural networks can be undertaken on many different levels. The biological neuron is itself a highly complex biochemical system that is still not entirely understood. Philosophers like John Searle [159] and Roger Penrose [141,142] argue that the intrinsic properties of the brain may not be modelled by any computer and that the human brain involves other mechanisms (e.g., quantum phenomenon). So far, no definite answer could be given and many a scientist believe that the brain computes within the Turing limit only.

Cognition and consciousness are phenomena that only appear on the highest level of abstraction in neural networks and there is probably no immediate correspondence between a given mental state and some neural network configuration.

Turing's neural networks must undoubtfully be situated between the most simple possible neural network models and they certainly abstract from almost all properties of the biological brain. Despite the neuron's elementariness, they exhibit many interesting and complex characteristics, as we shall see in this chapter.

5.1 General Properties

In this section, some basic properties and characteristics of Turing neural networks will be presented.

The simplest Turing network, the A-type machine, is built up from N neurons. A subset I of these neurons is used as input nodes. Each neuron, except the input neurons, receive input from exactly two other neurons. Thus, the number of interconnections in an A-type network is as follows:

Definition 5.1.1 (A-type network interconnections)
A network interconnection is defined as a directed edge that interconnects two neurons in a network. Thus, an A-type network with N neurons contains $2(N - I)$ interconnections. I is the number of input neurons. ∎

Remember the B-type link from Figure 2.6. This kind of link—which is, as already seen, itself a three-node A-type network—is built up from seven interconnections. According to Definition 5.1.1, there are $2(N - I)$ such three-node A-type networks in a B-type network (since a B-type network is constructed by replacing each interconnection in an A-type network by the three-node switch shown in Figure 2.6). Thus, the following proposition holds:

Proposition 5.1.1 (B-type network interconnections)
A B-type network is built up from $14(N - I)$ interconnections. ∎

The mindful reader has certainly already seen that a B-type network built up from N neurons contains in fact many more nodes because of the interconnection switches. Note, that when we talk about a N-neuron B-type machine, we talk about a machine built up from N "basic" neurons, without counting the link nodes. On the other hand, a D flip-flop with its preceding NAND gate is called "primitive" node. The total number of primitive nodes is given by the following proposition:

Proposition 5.1.2 (B-type network nodes)
A N-neuron B-type network is built up from $N + 6(N - I) = 7N - 6I$ primitive nodes. ∎

According to Figure 2.25, a TB-type interconnection switch is built up from four primitive nodes and nine interconnections (there are two incoming connections for the inverter node) The same is valid for TBI-type interconnection switches. Thus, the following propositions hold for TB-type and TBI-type networks:

Proposition 5.1.3 (TB-type and TBI-type network interconnections)
A N-neuron TB-type or TBI-type network contains $18(N - I)$ interconnections. I is the number of input neurons. ∎

Proposition 5.1.4 (TB-type and TBI-type network nodes)
A N-neuron TB-type or TBI-type network is built up from $N + 8(N - I) = 9N - 8I$ primitive nodes. ∎

Note also, that the number of links in Turing networks is linearly dependent on the number of neurons. Thus, simulations and implementations of large networks will not suffer from "exponential explosion".
Turing himself already put the following proposition:

Proposition 5.1.5 (Network equivalence)
Any B-type or BI-type network is an A-type network too [192, p. 11]. ∎

The proof is easy: since a B-type or BI-type machine is constructed from an A-type machine by replacing all directed edges by a three-node A-type machine as shown in Figure 2.6, the so obtained machine can be regarded as an A-type machine. The inverse statement, i.e., "All A-type machines are B-type machines" does not hold because it is extremely unlikely that one gets a B-type machine if one constructs an A-type machine randomly from a given number of nodes.

Neither BS-type nor BI1-type networks can be regarded as A-type networks since they use additional components. On the other hand, TB-type, TBI-type and CP-type networks might be regarded as A-type networks. Again, the inverse statement is not true.

Proposition 5.1.6 (Network equivalence)
Any TB-type, TBI-type, or CP-type network is an A-type network too. ∎

For any discrete machine, it is interesting to find out its states (or configurations). The number of states may be infinite, but enumerable. This kind of machinery is said to have *infinite memory* [192, p. 6]. Turing also gave a definition of the storage capacity of a machine with a finite number of possible states.

Definition 5.1.2 (Machine storage capacity)
A machine with a finite number of possible states N has a memory capacity of $log_2 N$ binary digits [192, p. 6]. ∎

For example, a N-node A-type machine has 2^N different possible configurations, i.e., 2^N possible states. According to Turing's definition, the memory capacity of such a machine is thus equal to $log_2(2^N) = N$ digits.

5.2 Computational Power

In Sections 2.2.4 and 2.3.6 the problem of universal computation has already been mentioned. Turing's vision of "educating" machines rather naively ended in the statement that his B-type networks could do any required job, given sufficient time and a sufficient number of neurons (see Section 2.2.4). Unfortunately, this statement was proven wrong (see Section 2.3.6): B-type and BI-type networks are not universal! Therefore, new kinds of universal networks, namely CP-type, TB-type, TBI-type, BS-type, and BI1-type networks, have been presented in Section 2.4.

The concept of *universal computation*, also called *Turing computation*, not only interested Turing (see also Section 5.11): today it has for example been proved for a number of neural network models that they are universal computers. It suffices to show that a universal Turing machine can be simulated by the according network. For example, J. Pollack [143] showed that a certain recurrent neural model—which he called a "neuring machine" for "neural Turing"—is universal. Franklin and Garzon [62] demonstrated in 1990 that any computable function can be computed via a suitable neural network. Then, in her 1991 paper, Siegelmann proved the following theorem:

Theorem 5.2.1 (Turing machines and recurrent neural networks)
Any Turing machine can be simulated with fully connected recurrent networks built on neurons with sigmoid activation functions [166].   ■

Later, Siegelmann and Sontag [167] established the existence of a network capable of simulating a finite-tape universal Turing machine in linear time.

"The construction results in a simulation of a Turing machine by a recurrent network which employs roughly 1000 neurons" [171].

Thus, a theoretically interesting question is whether a Turing machine can be simulated with a Turing neural network or not. Unfortunately, Turing did not give a formal proof of this hypothesis because "[...] it lies rather too far outside the main argument". However, from Section 2.3.6 we already know that a B-type machine cannot implement any boolean function, thus, it will not do any required job. But what about the newly proposed networks?

Proposition 3.3.1, for example, said that every logical function could be computed with a TB-type network. Thus, we know that from a theoretical point of view, a Turing machine could be realized, respectively simulated. It is "only" an engineering problem to implement the machine. In analogy to Theorem 5.2.1, the following theorem is valid:

Theorem 5.2.2 (TB-type and TBI-type Turing computability)
Any Turing machine can be simulated with a TB-type or TBI-type network.   ■

Note that the number of neurons has not been fixed during computation. It is assumed that, at any moment, as many neurons are available as necessary. An incomplete scratch of the proof for the above theorem has already be given in Section 3.6, where a shift-register (the Turing machine tape!) has been designed using a TB-type network. To get a Turing machine to work, however, a lot of engineering would still be necessary! But we know that it is possible since the primitive computational operators of TB-type and TBI-type networks form a logical basis.

Analogously, since BS-type and CP-type networks are universal and since TB-type and TBI-type networks can be regarded as A-type networks, the following theorems are valid:

Theorem 5.2.3 (BS-type and CP-type Turing computability)
Any Turing machine can be simulated with a BS-type or CP-type network.   ■

Theorem 5.2.4 (A-type Turing computability)
Any Turing machine can be simulated with an A-type network.   ■

To illustrate the above train of thought, let us make a short excursion to cellular automaton, namely to the *Game of Life*. The *Game of Life* is a well-known two-dimensional cellular automaton invented by Conway in the sixties. He wanted to design the most simple cellular automaton that supports universal computation. This was in some way a countercurrent to Von Neumann's extremely complicated self-reproducing cellular automaton. The cells of the *Game of Life* within their eight-cell neighbourhood can be either live or dead. "Lifelike" rules are used to describe the next state of a cell:

- A live cell dies if it has less than two live neighbors (loneliness) or if it has more than three neighbours (overcrowding).
- An dead cell becomes alive if it has three live neighbours (reproduction).
- A cell stays as it is if it has exactly two live neighbours (stasis).

The *Game of Life* became quite popular after the publication of an article in the Scientific American in 1970 [73]. Later on, Berlekamp et al. suggested that the *Game of Life* might be used to simulate a computer:

> "It is possible to construct AND, OR, and NOT gates using the *Game of Life*". [...] "From here on it's just an engineering problem to construct an arbitrary large, finite (and very slow!) computer" [22].

This proof seems rather weak, however, from a theoretical point of view it is sufficient. AND, OR, and NOT gates form a logical basis and it is thus possible to construct a computer or even a Turing machine. Berlekamp, however, only shows how the logical primitives might be implemented. To the best of my knowledge, nobody has ever implemented a working Turing machine by means of the *Game of Life*, however, it is commonly believed that such an "adventure" would be successful (besides its complete uselessness!).

5.3 State Machines

State machines are very important in digital systems design and are used in almost any complex digital circuit. Remember also that the head of a Turing machine is controlled by a state machine! A synchronous sequential state machine can be represented schematically by the circuit depicted in Figure 5.1.

Once in a particular state, the system must be capable of remaining in that state for some finite period of time even if the system inputs change. This requirement dictates memory capability for the state machine. Furthermore, the state machine must have a set of inputs and a set of outputs.

A state machine has a finite number I of inputs. The variables $x_1, x_2, ..., x_I$ are called *input variables*. Similarly, the machine has a finite number of O outputs. The output variables $z_1, z_2, ..., z_O$ are called *output variables*. The

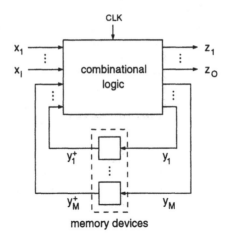

Fig. 5.1. Representation of a synchronous sequential state machine.

state memory is a set of M flip-flops that store the current state of the machine.

The next state of the machine is determined by the *next state function F* as a function of the current state and the input:

$$\text{Next state} = F(\text{current state, input}) \tag{5.1}$$

$$\text{Output} = G(\text{current state, input}) \tag{5.2}$$

State machines may use positive-edge-triggered D flip-flops for their state memory. A state machine whose output depends on both state and input is called a *Mealy machine*. In some sequential circuits the output depends on the state alone:

$$\text{Output} = G(\text{current state}) \tag{5.3}$$

Such a circuit is called a *Moore machine*. Obviously, the only difference between the two state-machine models is in how the outputs are generated. Thus, can we build a state machine with Turing networks?

In general, artificial neural networks are systems obtained from a finite number of memory-free scalar neurons and weighted interconnections. The complete system is updated synchronously in discrete time steps, and the transmission of information among neurons requires a unit time delay. Sontag noted: "In this formal sense, neural networks constitute a (very) particular type of automaton" [171]. The area of relations between automata and neural nets is an old one, dating back at least to the work of McCulloch and Pitts [119]. It is well-known that finite automata can be simulated with (recurrent) neural networks [171]. In Rojas [150, p. 44] for example, the interested reader may find the proof that any finite state automaton can be simulated with a network of McCulloch-Pitts units. Further interesting reading is Aleksander and Morton [5], both of whom introduced the *neural state machine* as a general model. I will not go into more details here.

It seems obvious that a state machine can be built with a Turing network. Nevertheless, let us look at this in more detail. As shown in Figure 5.1, one needs memory devices and a block of combinational logic. As each Turing neuron contains a D flip-flop (see Figure 2.3), we already dispose of the necessary memory devices. However, we can thus not build a "real" combinational system. But, as already stated in Section 3.1, a sequential system can be regarded as a combinational one when the clock frequency is sufficiently high compared to the changes of the input signals of the system.

Let us assume that the combinational logic of the state machine has a delay of T clock cycles. As a consequence, the memory devices must also have a delay of T clock cycles. This can simply be realized by putting in series T neurons. Figure 5.2 shows the fundamentals of a Turing net state machine implementation. Note that the machine processes data not at the speed of CLK but at the speed of T, the system clock. The advantage of such an implementation is that the state machine can be designed by means of well-known design methods (see for example Wakerly [206]) and hence does not contain useless parts.

In 1967, Minsky stated that every finite state machine can be simulated with some neural network:

> "Every finite-state machine is equivalent to, and can be 'simulated' by, some neural net. That is, given any finite-state machine M, we can build a certain neural net N^M which, regarded as a black-box machine, will behave precisely like M" [125].

Similarly, the same proposition is valid for universal Turing networks:

Proposition 5.3.1 (State machines and Turing networks)
Any finite automaton can be simulated with an A-type, a TB-type, a TBI-type, a CP-type, or a BS-type network.   ∎

A constructive proof has been given above. Note, that A-type, TB-type, TBI-type, CP-type, or BS-type networks might be used to building a state machine as depicted in Figure 5.2. One has just to be aware of the interconnection delays and of the interconnection switch states.

5.4 Threshold Logic

Threshold units, in their binary form first introduced by McCulloch and Pitts in 1943 [119], are a generalization of the common logic gates. It is astonishing

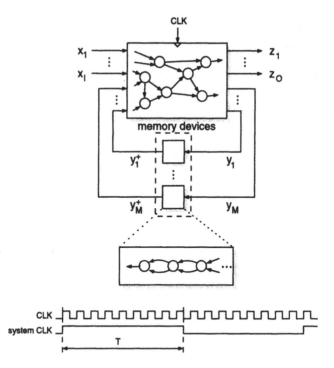

Fig. 5.2. Synchronous sequential state machine built up from Turing neurons.

that Turing makes no reference in his 1948 report to the work of McCulloch and Pitts [119]!

The basic function of a *linear threshold gate* (LTG) is to discriminate between vectors belonging to two different classes. A threshold element maps a vector of input data into a single binary output.

Definition 5.4.1 (Threshold element [104])
A threshold element, or gate, has n two-valued inputs $x_1, x_2, \ldots, x_n$ and a single-valued output y. Its internal parameters are a threshold T and weights $w_1, w_2, \ldots, w_n$ where each weight w_i is associated with a particular input variable x_i. The values of the threshold T and the weights w_i $(i = 1, 2, \ldots, n)$ may be any real, finite, positive or negative numbers. The input-output relation of a threshold element is defined as follows:

$$y = \begin{cases} 1 & \text{if and only if} \quad \sum_{i=1}^{n} w_i x_i \geq T \\ 0 & \text{if and only if} \quad \sum_{i=1}^{n} w_i x_i < T \end{cases} \tag{5.4}$$

where the sum and product operations are the conventional arithmetic ones. The sum $\sum_{i=1}^{n} w_i x_i$ is called the weighted sum of the element. ∎

A boolean function that can be realized with a single LTG is known as a *threshold function* [82]. Such a function is *linearly separable*, i.e., a function with inputs belonging to two distinct classes such that one class can be separated geometrically from the other by a hyperplane. Note that the XOR function is not a threshold function as it is not linearly separable.

McCulloch-Pitts networks are even simpler, as they are based on binary-valued signals only. Networks are composed of directed unweighted edges of *excitatory* and *inhibitory* type. Thereby, a 1 at an inhibitory synapse at the moment t unconditionally sets the output of the unit to 0 at time $t + 1$. Each McCulloch-Pitts unit is also provided with a certain threshold value T. The properties of McCulloch-Pitts networks lead us to the following two propositions:

Proposition 5.4.1 (McCulloch-Pitts nets and logical functions)
Any logical function $F : \{0,1\}^n \to \{0,1\}$ *can be computed with a McCulloch-Pitts network of two layers.*   ∎

Proposition 5.4.2 (McCulloch-Pitts nets and finite automaton)
Any finite automaton can be simulated with a McCulloch-Pitts network.   ∎

For both propositions, a constructive proof might be found in Rojas [150] or in Minsky [125].

As McCulloch-Pitts networks do not use weighted edges, the question of weather weighted networks are more general than unweighted ones must be answered. It can be seen that positive rational weights can be simulated by simply fanning-out the edges of the network the required number of times [150] (see Figure 5.3).

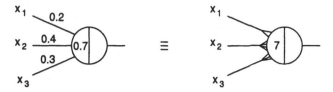

Fig. 5.3. A weighted network is equivalent to an unweighted one.

The same can be done in the case of irrational weights if the number of input vectors is finite. Rojas [150] also proved that networks with negative weights can be simulated using unweighted McCulloch-Pitts elements.

Normally, McCulloch-Pitts units produce the result without delay. However, for recurrent networks, a temporal factor in the computation can be introduced. Rojas stated:

"The numerical capabilities of any feed-forward network with instantaneous computation at the nodes can be reproduced by networks of units with delay. We only have to take care to coordinate the arrival of the input values at the nodes. This could make the introduction of additional computing elements necessary, whose sole mission is to insert the necessary delays for the coordinated arrival of information. This is the same problem that any computer with clocked elements has to deal with" [150].

Thus, the problems encountered with threshold logic are exactly the same as the problems with Turing networks (see Chapter 3, "Synthesis of Logical Functions and Digital Systems with Turing Networks")!

Threshold logic elements are more powerful than conventional logical gates. Kohavi stated: "Their higher capability is manifested by the ability of single threshold elements to realize a larger class of functions than is realizable by any one conventional gate" [104]. In fact, a threshold element can be considered as a generalization of the conventional gates because any of the latter can be realized by a single threshold element. For example, a two-input NAND gate can be realized by a single threshold element with weights -1, -1, and threshold $T = -1.5$. Note that is impossible to realize NAND or NOT gates using uninhibited McCulloch-Pitts units. For doing so, inhibitory connections are necessary.

One of the limitations of the practical usefulness of threshold logic is the lack of effective synthesis procedures. So far, there exists no satisfactory method allowing to determine the required number of elements, their weights, their thresholds, and their interconnections. In fact, exactly the same limitation is valid for Turing networks. Although, there are some differences between the boolean architectures of Turing and McCulloch-Pitts, but there is equivalence in the extended sense [39]. For example, inhibitory synapses are a primitive feature of McCulloch-Pitts nets, but not of Turing networks. Copeland and Proudfoot [39] propose to mimic an inhibitory synapse by an arrangement of three introverted pairs, one modified in such a way that each unit of the pair has an external input. On the other hand, an introverted pair can easily be simulated by McCulloch-Pitts units as shown in Figure 5.4. Each Turing node can be replaced by a two-unit McCulloch-Pitts network performing a NAND operation. Thus, any Turing network can be mimicked by a network of McCulloch-Pitts units. Working in the opposite direction, any McCulloch-Pitts network is equivalent to a logical function and can thus be simulated with a Turing network. This leads us to the following proposition:

Proposition 5.4.3 (McCulloch-Pitts and Turing nets)
Any network of McCulloch-Pitts units can be simulated with an A-type, a TB-type, a TBI-type, a CP-type, or a BS-type network. Any Turing network (including the non-universal nets) can be simulated with a McCulloch-Pitts network. ∎

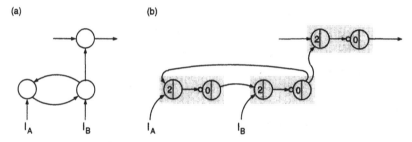

Fig. 5.4. Simulation of a Bl-type link (a) by McCulloch-Pitts units (b).

5.5 Dynamical Systems and the State-Space Model

In order to proceed with our study of Turing networks, we need a model that describes the dynamics of a network. A model which is naturally suited is the *state-space model*. According to this model, we think in terms of a set of *state variables* whose values at any particular instant of time are supposed to contain sufficient information to predict the future evolution of the system [84]. Let $d_1[t], d_2[t], ..., d_N[t]$ denote the state variables of our Turing network. Typically, the system state vector as shown in Equation 5.5 would be composed of the states of all nodes in a network (including the state of the link nodes).

$$\vec{d}[t] = \begin{bmatrix} d_1[t] \\ \vdots \\ d_N[t] \end{bmatrix} \qquad \text{(system state vector)} \tag{5.5}$$

The dynamics of a nonlinear dynamical system can be described by a first-order differential equation:

$$\frac{d}{dt}\vec{d}[t] = \vec{F}(\vec{d}[t]) \tag{5.6}$$

Equation 5.6 is also known as *state-space equation*. $\vec{F}(.)$ is the *state-transition function* that describes the state change in time. In our case, the dynamical system is a *discrete-time system*. Regardless of the exact form of the state-transition function, the state vector $\vec{d}[t]$ must vary with time t. Otherwise, the system is no longer dynamic since $\vec{d}[t]$ is constant. According to Haykin [84], a dynamical system might be defined as follows:

Definition 5.5.1 (Dynamical systems)
   A dynamical system is a system whose state varies with time.   ∎

As the system state vector of Turing neural networks varies with time, we conclude with the following corollary:

Corollary 5.5.2 (Dynamical systems)
Turing neural networks are dynamical systems.   ∎

Is a Turing neural network also a *nonlinear system*? Yes, in fact it is. The node transfer function ϕ (see Definitions 2.3.3 and 2.3.12) is a stepwise function and thus nonlinear. We conclude—what is intuitively obvious—the following:

Corollary 5.5.3 (Nonlinear dynamical systems)
Turing neural networks are nonlinear dynamical systems.   ∎

Complex systems are systems that are made up of "[...] many similar and simple parts" [57]. The behaviour of the simple parts (e.g., the Turing nodes) is easily understood, however, the behaviour of a system made up of many of such simple parts is "complex" and "[...] the future of complex systems cannot be predicted in the general case" [57]. Depending on their initial conditions, complex systems often behave completely differently and unpredictably. Since Turing networks are assembled by a set of very simple and similar elements, it can be concluded that:

Corollary 5.5.4 (Complex nonlinear dynamical systems)
Turing neural networks are complex nonlinear dynamical systems.   ∎

While simple systems subjected to random "forces" in general show a stochastic behaviour, complex systems can use the external noise to effect a transition from a chaotic regime to an ordered regime. Further details shall be given later in this book.

In the remainder of this chapter, we shall see many characteristics of nonlinear dynamical systems like chaotic behaviour, attractors, etc. But first, let us come back to the state-space model. Equation 5.6 describes the *motion* of a point in the N-dimensional state space. The state-space model is important because it allows us to visualize the dynamical system in order to analyze it. At a particular instant of time t, the state $\vec{d}[t]$ of the system can be represented by a single point in the N-dimensional state space. Changes in the state of the system are then represented as a curve in the state space. This curve is also called *trajectory* or *orbit* of the system [84].

Figure 5.5 shows a typical state-space trajectory of a 100-node TBI-type network. The trajectory has been projected into a three-dimensional space using the *principal components analysis (PCA)* method. As one can see, the network rapidly gets trapped in a fixed point attractor.

For different initial conditions, a family of trajectories results. This is referred to as the *state portrait* of the system. Given a state portrait of a dynamical system, one can construct the tangent vectors, i.e., the *velocity* for every point in the state space. This vector field is particularly useful in order to obtain a visual description of the tendency of the system to move.

For mathematical definitions of dynamical systems, stability and convergence, the interested reader is referred to Cook [35]. A summary is also given

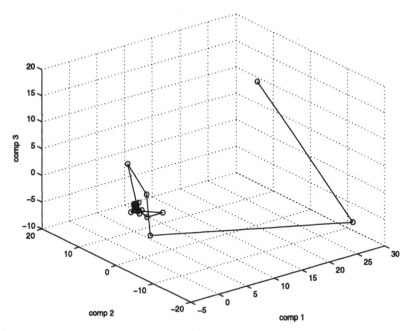

Fig. 5.5. State-space trajectory of a 100-node TB-type Turing neural network. The trajectory has been projected into a three-dimensional space using the PCA method. The network rapidly gets trapped in a fixed point attractor $(5, 10, -5)$.

in Haykin [84]. We shall be content with the rather intuitive definition of attractors given in Section 5.7.

Before going into more mathematical properties of Turing networks, I shall present in the next section a family of boolean networks that exhibit very similar properties to Turing networks.

5.6 Random Boolean Networks

Networks built of many interacting units, i.e., nodes and neurons, are used to study complex dynamical systems in may areas. *Random boolean networks (RBN)* form a class of networks in which the links between nodes and the boolean functions are specified at random. They are often specified by two parameters: N, the number of nodes and K, the number of incoming links per node (sometimes, K indicates the average number of links). *Synchronous random boolean networks* have been seriously investigated by Kauffman [99], Weisbuch [213] and others. RBN have for example been used as models for biological phenomena such as genetic regulatory networks. Further important work about boolean network dynamics came from Martland [114, 115, 117],

Amari [8,9], Rozonoér [154], and Derrida and Pomeau [50]. Practical systems for pattern classification with boolean networks have mainly been developed by Igor Aleksander [3,4,6].

Very little work has been done around *asynchronous random boolean networks (ARBN)*. Harvey and Bossomaier [80] have shown that they behave radically differently from the deterministic synchronous version. Earlier, Grondin et al. investigated the asynchronous behaviour of threshold-element networks and the role of deterministic chaos [76]. More recent work about rhythmic and non-rhythmic attractors in asynchronous random boolean networks comes from Di Paolo [137, 138]. Note, that for many physical and biological phenomena, the assumption of asynchrony seems more plausible.

Turing's unorganized machines might in fact be considered as a very particular subset of synchronous random boolean networks:

Proposition 5.6.1 (RBN and Turing nets)
Turing neural networks form a subclass of random boolean networks. Their boolean function is a NAND function and the number of incoming links is fixed to $K = 2$.   ∎

Remember from Section 5.1 that a N-neuron TBI-type network without input nodes is built up from $9N$ primitive nodes (D flip-flop with preceding NAND gate). As a direct consequence, a N-neuron TBI-type network should be considered a random boolean network made up of $9N$ boolean nodes!

A Turing unorganized machine can always be regarded as a random boolean network! The inverse statement is not true since it is very unlikely that one gets a Turing unorganized machine when randomly constructing a boolean network. Furthermore, compared to Turing nets (with the exception of A-type nets), Kauffman's random boolean networks do not allow an external agent to configure the network directly.

Kauffman's studies have revealed surprisingly ordered structures in randomly constructed networks. In particular, the most highly organized behaviour (i.e., small attractors, small number of attractors, stable attractors, etc.) appeared to occur in networks where each node—like in Turing's unorganized networks!—receives inputs from two other nodes ($K = 2$). It turned out that the networks exhibit three major regimes of behaviour:

1. *ordered* (solid),
2. *complex* (liquid), and
3. *chaotic* (gas).

The most complex and interesting dynamics correspond to the liquid interface, the boundary between order and chaos. In the ordered regime, little computation can occur. In the chaotic phase, dynamics are too disordered to be useful. The most important and dominant results of Kauffman's numerical simulations can be summarized as follows [99] (note that attractors will be further discussed in Section 5.7):

- The expected median state cycle length is about $\sqrt{N}$ (where N is the number of network nodes).
- Most networks have short state cycles, while a few have very long ones.
- The number of state cycle attractors is about $\sqrt{N}$. Therefore, a random boolean network with 10,000 elements would be expected to have in the order of 100 alternative attractors. A system with 100,000 would have about 317 alternative asymptotic attractors.
- The most interesting dynamics appear with an average connectivity of $K = 2$ (the "edge of chaos").
- State cycles are inherently stable to most minimal transient perturbations.
- A perturbed state cycle can directly change only to a small number of other state cycle attractors in the system.

The last item partially explains the difficulties encountered for the pattern classification tasks presented in Section 4.5. Even when the inputs of a classifier network change, it is not possible to jump into any other attractor.

In his recent book [101], Stuart Kauffman presents new investigations around random boolean networks. For example, he shows that random boolean networks in the ordered regime have a power law distribution of avalanches in gene activities produced by reversing the activity of a single randomly chosen gene. On the other hand, in the chaotic regime, in addition to the power law distribution of avalanches, a large spike of vast avalanches appears that affects $30 - 50\%$ of the genes. Furthermore, he shows that networks with more than $K = 2$ inputs per node can be shifted into the ordered regime from the chaotic regime by choosing appropriate, so called "canalizing" boolean functions.

For further details, the interested reader is referred to [99, 101].

5.7 Attractors

An *attractor* in a dynamical system is an *equilibrium state*. Each attractor is encompassed by a *bassin (domain) of attraction*. A deterministic complex dynamical system with a finite number of states ultimately "settles down" in an attractor after a finite time. If the state vector comes to rest completely, it is called a *fixed point*. If the state vector settles into a periodic motion, it is called a *limited cycle*. There also exists *chaotic* or *strange* attractors. Thereby, the state vector moves chaotically, in the sense that two copies of the system which initially have nearly identical states will grow more and more dissimilar as they evolve [87].

As presented in the previous section, Kauffman has shown that the expected median state cycle length in random boolean networks is about $\sqrt{N}$ and that the number of state cycle attractors is about $\sqrt{N}$ too. The question is whether these values are also valid for Turing's neural networks. Figures 5.6 and 5.7 show two typical plots that arise when drawing the attractor length and the number of attractors of a TBI-type network in function of the number of network nodes. For comparison, $\sqrt{N}$ is also plotted on the drawing. One can see that the number of attractors as well as the attractor length approximatively follow $\sqrt{N}$. Additionally, Figure 5.8 shows a histogram of the number of attractors in function of the attractor length for a 100-node TBI-type network.

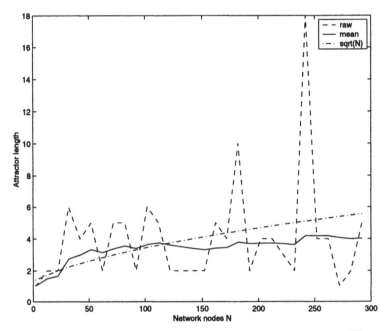

Fig. 5.6. Attractor length of a TBI-type network. The value is about $\sqrt{N}$.

Figure 5.9 shows the state-space trajectory of a $K = 4$ (four incoming links per node) TBI-type network made up of 100 nodes. The network falls into a limited cycle attractor. A fixed point attractor has already been shown in Figure 5.5.

In order to obtain a system that adapts, classifies and generalizes, attractors are necessary. However, in absence of any further ordering principle, attractors are generally chaotic. The goal of learning (network "organizing") is for the most part the generation of non-chaotic attractors.

Ross Asbhy—a major contributor to the field of cybernetics—was one of the first to examine the concept of adaptation as an adaptive walk in the parameter space of a dynamical system towards parameter values that correspond to a dynamical system with "good" attractors [13]. His essential idea was mainly that a subset of the system's internal variables constitutes essential variables, which must be maintained within certain bounds. If the system

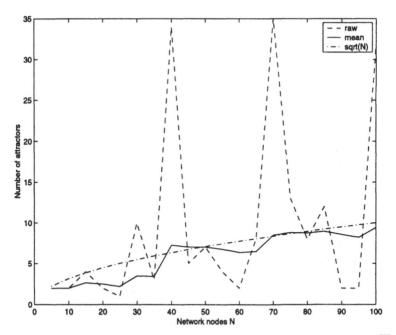

Fig. 5.7. Number of attractors of a TBI-type network. The value is about $\sqrt{N}$.

on the attractor kept the essential variables in bounds, change nothing. If the essential variables are not kept in bounds, however, then make a jump change in one of the parameters of the system that alters the state transitions and hence alters the bassins of attraction. Based on this idea, Asbhy was able to build a crude autopilot, called *homeostat*, which learned to hold an airplane in straight and level flight prior to crashing despite being wired at random to the controls.

The idea of adaptation is thus simply a walk in parameter space seeking good attractors. In the case of Turing's unorganized TBI-type machines, the only parameters that are modifiable are the switches of the interconnections between the neurons. A learning algorithm has thus to set the internal interconnection switches to values that enable the system to perform a given task—in other words, to tune the attractors of the networks. The walk in parameter space can be seen as hill climbing towards networks with desired attractors.

Kauffman also found out that *NK* family random boolean networks have rugged landscapes which trap adaptive walks. The following general features are important [99]:

- Network improvement is rapid at first and then slows and typically appears to stop.
- Walks often stop at local optima well below the global optimum.

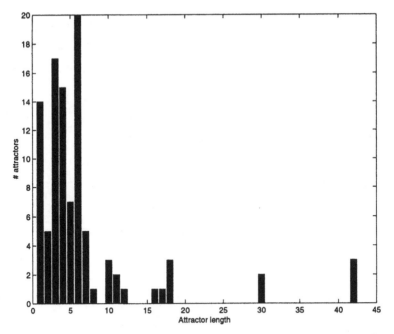

Fig. 5.8. Histogram of the number of attractors in function of the attractor length for a 100-node TBI-type network.

- Adaptive walks typically cannot achieve arbitrary patterns of activities on attractors.

The same characteristics seem valid for Turing networks too. Almost all fitness graphs in Section 4.5 show that the network fitness grows fast first and then slows down or even stops. Unsuccessful experiments have shown that the adaptive walk gets trapped in a local optima. However, sometimes the global optima can easily be reached when the experiments are initialized with new initial conditions.

Let us conclude with Turing himself in this section. He was obviously aware that the behaviour of his networks might be very complex: "However, machines of this character [i.e., A-type nets] can behave in a very complicated manner when the number of units is large" [192, p. 10]. As we will see in the next few sections, he was certainly right!

5.8 Network Stability and Activity

In his 1971 paper, Amari [8] investigated the characteristics of networks composed of randomly connected threshold elements with the intention of understanding some aspects of information processing in nervous systems.

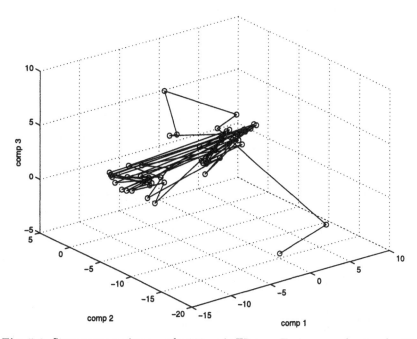

Fig. 5.9. State-space trajectory of a 100-node TB-type Turing neural network with four incoming links per node ($K = 2$). The trajectory has been projected into a three-dimensional space using the PCA method. The network falls into a limited cycle attractor.

His networks—called RATEN (random threshold-element network)—are considered networks whose weights and thresholds are random variables. Complex systems are obtained by interconnecting RATENs in a random manner. Mathematically speaking, a RATEN is not an actual network but a probability space consisting of an infinite number of sample networks (a sample space), an algebra of sets of networks, and a probability measure in it [9]. Actual networks are just samples of a RATEN. Amari was able to show that two statistical parameters are sufficient to determine the characteristics of the networks. He further categorized the networks by these parameters into three classes:

1. *monostable networks,*
2. *bistable networks,* and
3. *astable networks.*

Networks are called monostable if they only have one stable level, they are called bistable if they have exactly two stable levels, and they are called astable when they do not converge to an equilibrium level.

The threshold element is a universal logical element in the sense that any boolean function can be realized by threshold elements only (see also Section 5.4). The boolean-logical method of approach, however, seems to be insufficient to understand the macroscopic characteristics of a large-scale system of threshold elements [8]. Amari investigated large-scale networks from the macroscopic point of view. From a macroscopic point of view, information is not carried by each of the boolean outputs of the components independently but by a real-valued function of them. The activity level which designates the percentage of exciting elements is such a function. He considered that the statistical quantities concerning the connection weights and the threshold values of the elements are sufficient to explain the macroscopic characteristics of networks.

In analogy with the above descriptions, a Turing network might also be considered as a sort of RATEN where the connections are enabled or disabled at random. Like Turing networks, RATENs are also updated synchronously at fixed time intervals, however, the interconnections of a RATEN are different from Turing nets: "The interconnection is performed in such a manner that the output x_i of an element T_i is fed back to the ith inputs of all the elements" [8].

Besides Kauffman and Weisbuch, D. Martland also investigated the behaviour of boolean networks [115, 117]. The following network activity and the network stability definitions are inspired by Martland and Amari's work.

Definition 5.8.1 (Network activity level)
The network activity level L is defined as the average value of all computing elements.

$$L = \frac{1}{D} \sum_{i=1}^{D} x_i \qquad x_i \in \{0, 1\} \qquad (5.7)$$

$D = N - I$ is the number of computing elements in a network. If the network has no inputs, then $D = N$. The activity level satisfies $0 \leq L \leq 1$. If $L = 1$, all the nodes are excited, i.e., $\forall i \in \{1...D\}, x_i = 1$. The activity level of a net indicates the percentage of the components excited (set to 1). For very large networks, L may be treated as a continuous quantity. ∎

The network activity level can be used to classify networks into the three classes seen above.

Definition 5.8.2 (Stability criteria for Turing networks)
A Turing network is called stable, when every activity level converges to an equilibrium level, and called astable, when there exists an activity level which does not converge to any equilibrium level. A stable network is called monostable, when it has one and only one stable level, and called bistable, when it has exactly two stable levels. ∎

Following Martland, the network stability S is defined as follows:

Definition 5.8.3 (Network stability)
Given a N-node binary network. For any two states s_i and s_k, the network stability s is defined by:

$$S = \frac{Hamming\ distance\ (s_i, s_k)}{|s_i|} = \frac{(|s_i - s_k|) \cdot (|s_i - s_k|}{|s_i|} \tag{5.8}$$

The network stability is equal to the number of bits the two state vectors differ by, divided by the length of the state vector. ∎

The following definitions are introduced to classify and characterize Turing neural networks:

Definition 5.8.4 (Network output activity level)
The network output activity level o is defined as the average value of all O output elements.

$$o = \frac{1}{O} \sum_{i=1}^{O} x_i \qquad x_i \in \{0, 1\} \tag{5.9}$$

The activity level satisfies $0 \leq o \leq 1$. If $o = 1$, all the output nodes are excited, i.e., $\forall i \in \{1...O\}, x_i = 1$. The activity level indicates the percentage of the components excited (set to 1). ∎

The activity level does not describe the dynamics of a network. Therefore, I introduce the *node activity* and the *network activity*:

Definition 5.8.5 (Node activity)
Let E be the number of intervals (clock cycles) the networks has been run for and let C be the number of times a node changed its value. The node activity a is defined as

$$a = \frac{C}{E}. \tag{5.10}$$

The node activity satisfies $0 \leq a \leq 1$. When $a = 0$ the node never changed its value, when $a = 1$, the node always changed its value. ∎

The node activity can be interpreted as an indicator of the *node stability*. A high activity indicates that the node often changed its value.

Definition 5.8.6 (Network activity)
Let E be the number of intervals (clock cycles) the networks has been run for, C_i the number of times the node i changed its value, and D the number of computing nodes. The network activity A is defined as

$$A = \frac{1}{D} \sum_{i=1}^{D} \frac{C_i}{E} = \frac{1}{D} \sum_{i=1}^{D} a_i \qquad (5.11)$$

whereas a_i is the activity of node $i \in \mathcal{D}$. The network activity satisfies $0 \leq A \leq 1$. When $A = 1$, each network node changed its value during each time interval (clock cycle).   ∎

Amari [9] noted that "[...] it is extremely difficult to analyze the behaviour of nets of threshold elements in general, and we are yet far from a full understanding of information-processing capabilities of nets of threshold elements". I am conscious that the above described characteristics are only an attempt to describe certain characteristics of Turing networks. Even though Turing networks are simpler than threshold networks, they are difficult to analyze.

In the next few sections, examples of some complex Turing network behaviours shall be presented.

5.8.1 Activity in A-type Networks

In this section, a series of experiments with A-type networks will be presented. The goal was to investigate the network activities of this simplest kind of network. A rather small network with $N = 100$ nodes has been chosen (mainly for computational limitations).

Eight experiments have been performed in the following way: First, a random A-type network with $N = 100$ network nodes, $O = 10$ output nodes, and $I \in [1, 4, 16, 25, 36, 49, 64, 81]$ input nodes has been built. All I input nodes became assigned a random value, all other nodes were set to 0. Then, the network was run for 100 clock cycles and the network activity, the output activity, and the network activity level were plotted in function of the number of clock cycles. Figures 5.10 to 5.18 show the plots obtained.

Let me briefly describe now the main characteristics that can be observed. Figure 5.10 shows the activity for a random network with one input only. It can be seen that, after approximatively 20 steps, the entire network has become completely bistable, i.e., the activity level oscillates between 1 (100%) and 0 (0%). Output and network activities quickly progress towards 1. Remember that all network nodes were initialized to 0. The only input has almost no influence on the entire network and even when its value is 1, it is certainly quickly "absorbed". The network then simply oscillates between 1 and 0 due to the NAND function implemented in all nodes.

Figures 5.11 to 5.13 still show bistable networks. Again, output and network activities progress towards 1. However, the reader can see that the network activity level oscillates within smaller values, e.g., between 0.4 and 0.9 in Figure 5.12. This means that parts of the networks are stable now. Note, that Figure 5.13 shows an interesting case where the network activity increases at the beginning, then decreases, and again increases.

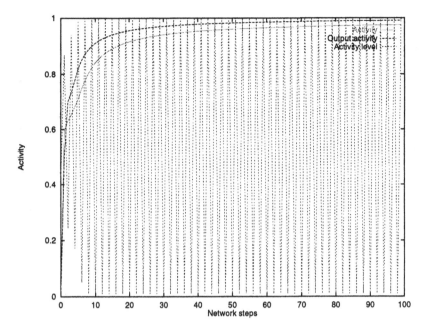

Fig. 5.10. Typical activities of a 100-node A-type network with 1 input node.

Next, Figure 5.14 shows a network where only about 0.1 of the neurons are bistable. As a consequence, the network and output activities progress towards 0.1. Figures 5.15 and 5.17 even show networks that are monostable after a short initial astable phase. As a consequence of the stable activity level, the network and output activities progress towards 0. Finally, Figures 5.16 and 5.18 have astable parts (the activity level oscillates!).

In summary, if the network activity decreases asymptotically towards 0, the network is or will become monostable. On the the other hand, if the activity progresses asymptotically towards 1, the network is or will become bistable or even astable. Figure 5.16, for example, shows a network where the output activity of the ten output nodes decreases towards zero. Thus, the output nodes are monostable and their values do not change. However, the network activity remains constant at about 0.12 (12%) which means that a part of the network is still astable. A network that has a constant activity is always partially bistable or astable.

The above presented experiments suggest that a certain "energy", represented as the number of randomly initialized input nodes, is required to perturbate the actual state of a network. This corresponds to Kauffman's observation that the networks are inherently stable to most minimal perturbations. However, if many inputs are connected to many network nodes, the network leaves its $0 - 1 - 0 - 1 - \ldots$ state cycle and could eventually get trapped in another attractor (see for example Figure 5.17). Further exper-

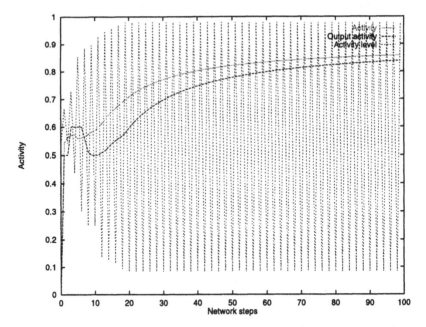

Fig. 5.11. Typical activities of a 100-node A-type network with 4 input nodes.

iments with very large networks (1,000,000 nodes!) have revealed the same behaviour.

5.8.2 Activity in BS-type Networks

Remember from Section 2.4.4 the newly proposed machine with special interfering links. I performed various experiments with BS-type networks too in order to investigate their network activities. This time, I have run the experiments with a network built up by 10,000 nodes. Again, the network was run for 100 clock cycles. The network had two dedicated output nodes only and no input nodes.

At the beginning, each node has been set to 0. This time, the number of enabled links was variable from $0 - 100\%$, and the enabled links were chosen at random. Again, the network was run for 100 clock cycles.

Figures 5.19 to 5.22 show the results obtained. Furthermore, Table 5.1 summarizes the activity results of this experiment.

For networks up to 70% of enabled links, the activity level is constant and the network activity thus decreases. These networks are all monostable after a certain time. Figure 5.19 shows the plot obtained for a network with 10% enabled connections. Figure 5.19 shows an interesting case. The network activity level is first oscillating, but becomes stable after about 60 clock cycles. Seventy percent of enabled connections seems to be a critical value since Figure 5.21 already shows a different behaviour. Network and output activities

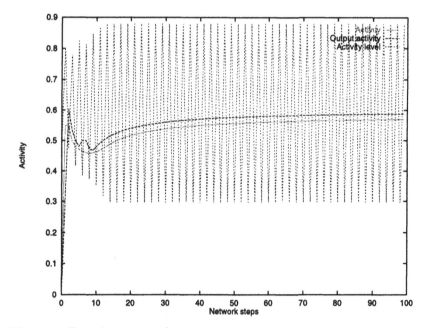

Fig. 5.12. Typical activities of a 100-node A-type network with 9 input nodes.

Enabled connections (100% = 20,000)	Stability	Network activity level
0%	monostable	0%
10%	monostable	16%
20%	monostable	27%
30%	monostable	35%
40%	monostable	41%
50%	monostable	46%
60%	monostable	50%
70%	monostable	54%
80%	bistable	11 − 92%
90%	bistable	2 − 98%
100%	bistable	0 − 100%

Table 5.1. Summary of the BS-type activity experiments.

no longer decrease towards 0 but increase towards 1. Furthermore, networks with more than about 70% of enabled connections become bistable.

The same experiments were also performed with random initial node values. However, it turned out that the initial node values are of absolutely no importance to the general stability tendency (monostable or bistable/astable) of the network.

In order to find the exact point of inflection between network astability and monostability, I performed further experiments. First, I plotted the network activity in function of the number of enabled network connections.

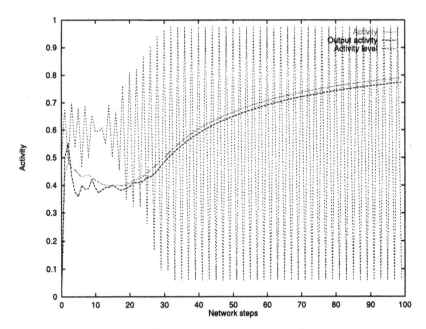

Fig. 5.13. Typical activities of a 100-node A-type network with 16 input nodes.

Thereby, since most networks are bistable (or even astable), I have drawn the minimum and the maximum network activity level of two consecutive network states. Thus, when minimum and maximum levels are equal, the network is monostable. On the other hand, when they get separated, the network is bistable or astable.

The result obtained is quite exciting and is shown in Figure 5.23. When I first saw it, a *bifurcation diagram* immediately came to my mind! Figure 5.24 shows a zoom into Figure 5.23 from 65 − 90% of enabled connections.

It can be seen that the network is monostable up to about 70% of enabled connections. Then, from 70% on, it seems to behave rather chaotically! If we zoom into the plot (see Figure 5.24), it can be seen that there exist, like in a bifurcation diagram, stable states (possibly attractors) for certain network states.

So far, all experiments were performed using 100 network steps for each activity measure. In order to have a closer and more precise view on the network behaviour, I ran the network for 1,000 steps and with a higher resolution (step size). The network was still built from 10,000 nodes. A step size of 0.0001 has been chosen, that means that the connections are enabled in two steps since there are 20,000 connections. Figure 5.25 shows the same results as already shown previously, but with a better resolution. It is interesting to see that the network is monostable up to about 65% of enabled connections. From 65 − 80%, there is a zone of chaotic dynamics and astability. This zone

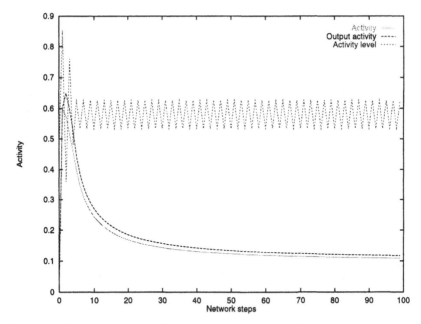

Fig. 5.14. Typical activities of a 100-node A-type network with 25 input nodes.

is followed by a zone of non-chaotic astability. Figure 5.26 zooms into a narrow zone from 77 − 79% of enabled connections. At least in three different places, the minimal and maximal activities get very close and the network thus reaches a monostable state within chaotic astability.

5.8.3 Activities in TB-type and TBI-type Networks

Just in order to make sure that a TB-type or TBI-type network behaves in the same way as the previously analyzed A-type and BS-type networks, I also performed an activity analysis for them. Figure 5.27 shows that TB-type networks behave in about the same way as A-type and BS-type nets. It can be concluded that the nodes within a TB-type link—adding additional delays—do not change the global stability behaviour of the network.

Figure 5.28 plots the network activity level as well as the network stability in function of the number of closed interconnections switches. The more connections are closed (enabled), the higher the activity and the stability become. This seems quite obvious since a highly interconnected network (i.e., a lot of enabled interconnections) transmits the node states further and to more neighbourhood nodes than a sparsely connected network. Thus, the network stability is higher, i.e., the state vector underlies more changes between two succeeding states. A highly interconnected network also results in a higher node-activity since a given node can be excited from more neighbourhood nodes.

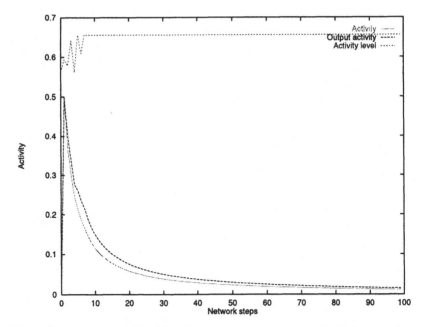

Fig. 5.15. Typical activities of a 100-node A-type network with 36 input nodes.

5.9 Chaos, Bifurcation, and Self-Organized Criticality

Indeed, the behaviour of Turing's networks is amazing and suggests a more detailed analysis of the inherent dynamics. Wang and Blum [210] investigated the dynamics and bifurcation of neural networks. Bifurcation is mainly concerned with how the network dynamics change as parameters are varied. Bifurcation and dynamics analysis of neural networks is related to the fundamental problem in recurrent neural networks on how to design attractors and their bassins of attraction such that the dynamics of the networks lead to transitions among the attractors. On the other hand, bifurcations in dynamical systems are a good indicator for the presence of chaos [74]. If the parameter space is divided by many bifurcations, the system becomes increasingly sensitive to initial conditions and small parameter changes: in other words, the system's behaviour becomes chaotic.

Deterministic chaos is different in principle from what is commonly known as random dynamics. Randomness is generally used to describe the nondeterministic nature of systems. With random dynamics prediction is intrinsically impossible, except in the statistical sense. The important characteristics of chaos are the apparent irregularity of time traces and the divergence of the trajectories over time in a system that is deterministic [74]. Flake states that "[p]rior to the discovery of chaos, determinism and randomness were believed to be mutually exclusive principles. Today, we know that this is not the case" [57]. Chaos is typically a phenomenon that is random even

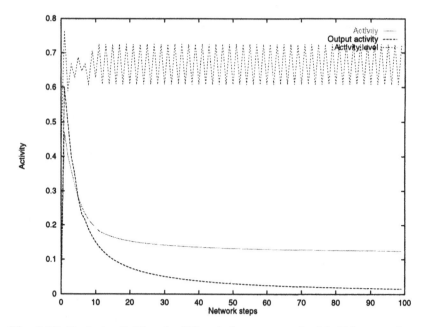

Fig. 5.16. Typical activities of a 100-node A-type network with 49 input nodes.

though it is deterministic. However, under some special cases, chaos can be seen to be equivalent to stochastic randomness. Chaotic systems are systems that are close to systems that can compute. Christopher Langton [111] and Stuart Kauffman [99] both like to talk about "computation at the edge of chaos". Flake states that "[...] whenever a dynamical system is shown to be capable of universal computation, the dynamical system possesses, at least in part, chaotic dynamics. This duality of chaos and computability is primarily a result of the recursive nature of dynamical systems and computing devices" [57]. Note, that "computation" is used in a loose sense and simply means that the information exchange between elements of the systems is maximized.

Chaos has also been observed and investigated in the brain (see for example Freeman [63], Guevara et al. [78], Skarda and Freeman [169], and Goldberger et al. [75]) and it is believed that it plays an important role in information processing.

The bifurcation-like activity plots presented in the previous sections directly suggest that Turing's neural networks exhibit chaotic behaviour as observed in many artificial and natural neural systems.

Large interactive systems (e.g., Turing neural networks) naturally evolve towards a *critical state* in which a minor change in the system can lead in turn towards a catastrophic avalanche of changes. *Self-organized criticality* is a concept first investigated by Per Bak and his colleagues [18,19]. Repeated

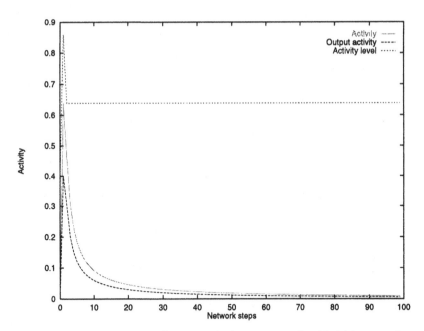

Fig. 5.17. Typical activities of a 100-node A-type network with 64 input nodes.

addition of sand at random positions to a sand pile causes avalanches of different sizes. Measuring the size distribution of the avalanches revealed a power law distribution: many small and few large avalanches. In his recent book [101], Stuart Kauffman revealed self-organized critical behaviour of *NK* co-evolutionary models.

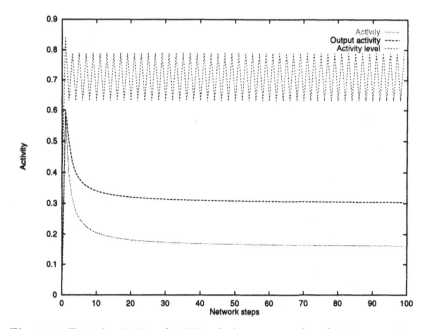

Fig. 5.18. Typical activities of a 100-node A-type network with 81 input nodes.

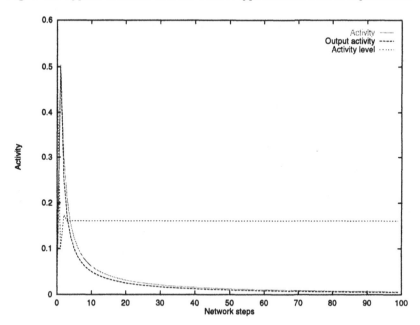

Fig. 5.19. Typical activity of a BS-type network with 10% of enabled links.

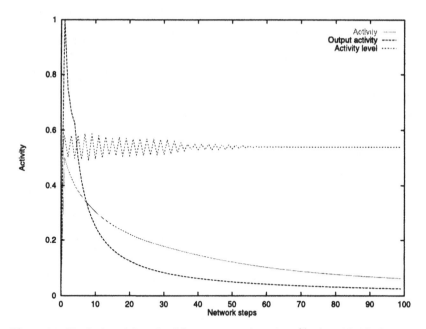

Fig. 5.20. Typical activity of a BS-type network with 70% of enabled links.

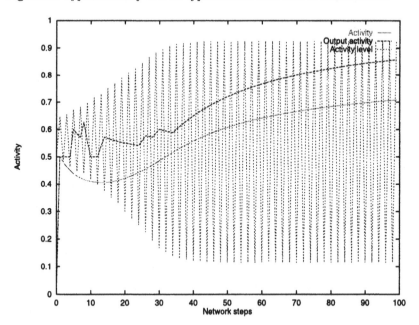

Fig. 5.21. Typical activity of a BS-type network with 80% of enabled links.

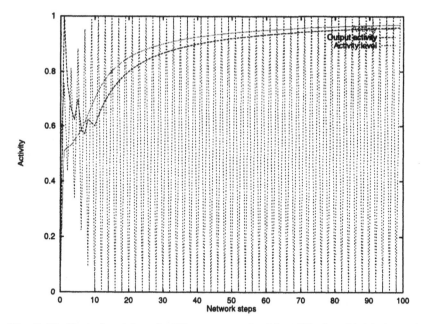

Fig. 5.22. Typical activity of a BS-type network with 100% of enabled links.

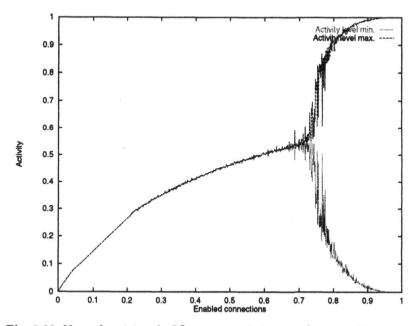

Fig. 5.23. Network activity of a BS-type network drawn in function of the number of enabled connections. Step size: 10 connections.

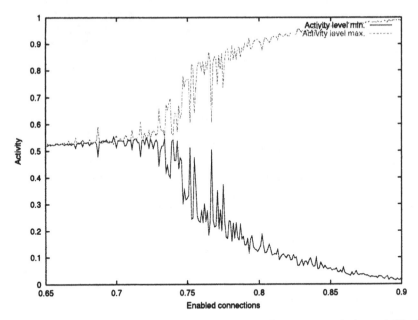

Fig. 5.24. Zoom into the network activity of a BS-type network (65 − 90% of enabled connections). Step size: 10 connections.

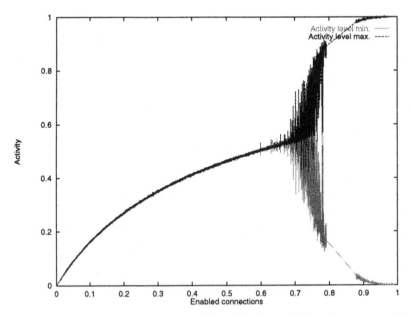

Fig. 5.25. Network activity of a BS-type network drawn in function of the number of enabled connections. Step size: 2 connections.

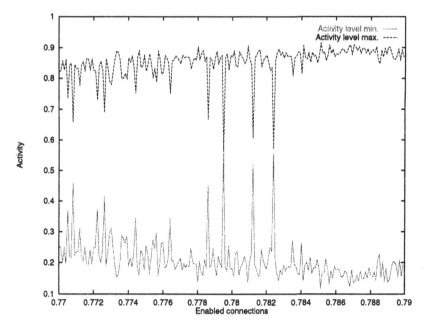

Fig. 5.26. Zoom into the network activity of a BS-type network (77 − 79% of enabled connections). Step size: 2 connections.

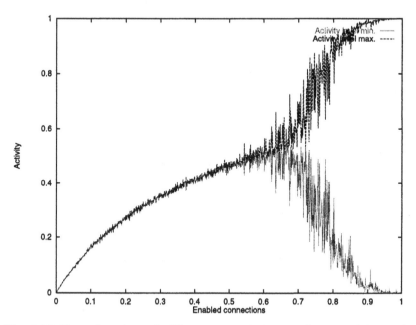

Fig. 5.27. Network activity of a TB-type network drawn in function of the number of enabled connections. Step size: 20 connections.

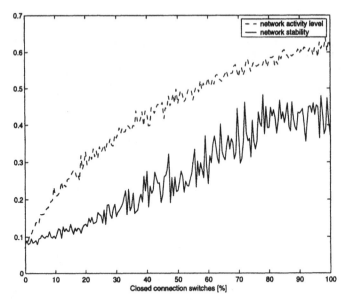

Fig. 5.28. Network activity level and network stability in function of the number of closed interconnection switches. Step size: 10 connections.

5.10 Topological Evolution and Self-Organization

Self-organization is a sort of unsupervised learning where a system is modified in accordance with prescribed rules. The key question, of course, is how a useful system configuration can finally develop from self-organization. The answer lies essentially in the following observation made by Turing [191]:

"Global order can arise from local interactions".

This observation is of fundamental importance and it applies to the brain and to artificial neural networks [84]. In particular, many originally random local interactions between neighbouring neurons of the network can coalesce into states of global order. Haykin [84] noted that network organization takes place at two different levels: *activity* and *connectivity*. Certain activity patterns are produced by a given network in response to the input signals. On the other hand, the network's connection strengths (or synaptic weights) are modified in response to neuronal signals in the activity patterns. The feedback between changes in synaptic weights and changes in activity patterns must be *positive* in order to achieve self-organization (instead of stabilization) of the network.

Topological evolution of dynamical networks has been studied in a recent paper by Bornholdt and Rohlf [24]. They evolved network topologies of an asymmetrically connected threshold network by a simple local rewiring rule: quiet nodes grow links, active nodes lose links. They have shown that this leads to an average connectivity of the networks towards the *critical* value $K_C = 2$ for large systems.

Kauffman postulated that gene regulatory networks may exhibit properties of complex dynamical networks near criticality [99], but, without providing an algorithm able to generate an topology near the critical point. Bornholdt and Rohlf asked "[...] whether connectivity may be driven towards a critical point by some dynamical mechanism" [24] and presented an approach that evolves the connectivity towards the critical point. In the remainder of this section we present a self-organizing topology evolving rule adapted for Turing's boolean networks that might also be applied to random boolean networks.

As we have seen in Section 2.4.3, each link between two nodes of a TBI-type network is equipped with a small A-type machine that functions as a switch (see Figure 2.26). When the switch is opened no information is passed, when it is closed all information is passed and inverted. So far, all networks had an connectivity of exactly $K = 2$ connections per node. Algorithm 4 presents one of several possible iterating rules that evolves the average connectivity of TBI-type networks towards the critical point. Instead of creating and removing interconnections, the algorithm only operates the switches incorporated in each link and thus *configures* the network topology. The connectivity $K(i)$ of a given node i is equivalent to the number of incoming links that have closed switches. At the end of a successful topology evolution, links with opened switches might simply be removed.

Algorithm 4 Topology evolution of TBI-type networks

Choose a fully connected network ($K = N$).
Choose a random switch configuration with an average connectivity K_{ini}.
for $t = 1$ to T time steps **do**
  Choose a random initial state vector $s(0)$.
  Find a dynamical attractor and determine its length L.
  for $l = 1$ to L **do**
    Run the network and record the activity $A(i)$ of each node.
  end for
  for all nodes i **do**
    if $A(i) = 0$ **then**
      A switch on link l_{ji} (where node j is chosen at random) is enabled/closed.
    else
      A switch on link l_{ji} (where node j is chosen at random) is disabled/opened.
    end if
  end for
end for

The activity $A(i)$ of a node i is defined as the number of changes it makes in the time interval $T_2 - T_1$. When Algorithm 4 is applied to a TBI-type network, a typical picture as shown in Figure 5.29 arises. The network self-organizes towards an average connectivity of about $K = 2.5$ ($N = 30$ nodes, 10^3 time steps), independent of the initial connectivity (switch configuration). For the simulations we ran, the average connectivity approximatively obeys the scaling law presented by Bornholdt and Rohlf [24]: $K_{ev}(N) - 2 = cN^{-\delta}$ where $c = 12.4$ and $\delta = 0.47$. Thus, when $N \to \infty$, the network evolves towards the critical connectivity $K_C = 2$. Figure 5.30 ($N = 30$ nodes, 10^3 time steps) shows the evolution of the average attractor length and the average number of attractors when Algorithm 4 is applied to a network. It can be seen that both values essentially remain constant. It is of a particular interest that, although Turing TBI-type networks are quite different compared to the asymmetrically connected threshold networks presented in [24], both models evolve towards the same critical connectivity $K_C = 2$ for large systems. Already Kauffman experimentally showed that the most interesting dynamics of random boolean networks appear with an average connectivity of $K = 2$ (the boundary between order and chaos!) [99]. However, he did not self-organize the topology of his networks.

Figure 5.31 shows the evolution of the switch states of a 30-node TBI-type network. The topological evolution started with all switches closed (closed=black). The algorithm rapidly opens a lot of switches (step $0 - 50$) because of the very high activity most nodes exhibit.

The above topology evolution algorithm (Algorithm 4) presents a new and different type of mechanism compared to the phenomenon of self-organized criticality [19]. The networks self-organize towards criticality and "[...] exhibit considerable robustness against noise in the system" [24]. Bornholdt and Rohlf have shown that the mechanism is based on a topological phase

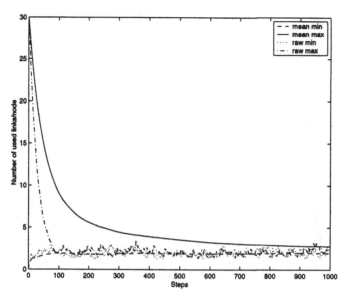

Fig. 5.29. Evolution of the average connectivity of a TBI-type network ($N = 30$ nodes).

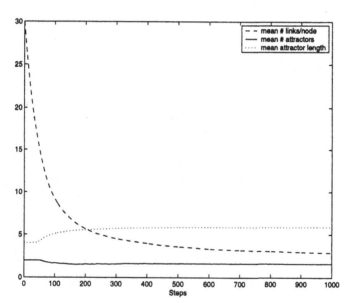

Fig. 5.30. Typical average attractor length and average number of attractors during TBI-type topology evolution ($N = 30$ nodes). Self-organization started at $K = 30$ (all connection switches closed).

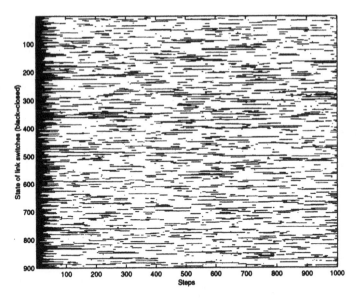

Fig. 5.31. Evolution of the switch states of a 30-node TBl-type network. The topological evolution started with all switches closed (closed=black).

transition in the networks. The crucial question is "[...] whether a comparable mechanism may occur in natural complex systems" [24]. Bornholdt and Rohlf further state "[...] that this form of global evolution of a network structure towards criticality might be found in natural complex systems". So far, there are still a lot of open questions. Kauffman's gene regulation networks are a good example of a biologically plausible model. It is still one of the greatest mysteries how the genetic code influences the development and growth of organisms. The synaptic changes in the brain are another example where the connectivity of a neural system is regulated.

So far, I only applied topology evolution to networks that had no particular task to complete. However, it would certainly be of great interest to investigate the evolution of the average number of links per node for networks that do a certain job. Remember the pattern recognition Example 4.6.2 from Section 4.6. This classification job was done with classical A-type and BS-type networks that exactly have $K = 2$ incoming links per node. In the following experiment, the number of incoming links per node has also been encoded on the genome. Each node could thus have zero up to N incoming links, which considerably enlarges the search space, i.e., the number of possible network architectures. Figure 5.32 shows the fitness graph obtained for a 1,000-node TB-type network. The network was able to correctly classify all twenty 16×16-dot patterns into the two possible classes. What about the number of links per node? Figure 5.33 shows the evolution of the number of incoming links per node. For each generation, the number of incoming links is plotted for the best individual and on the average (for the entire population). It can be seen that the best individual (that was able to find a solution to the problem) has an interconnectivity of about $K = 2$ incoming links per node! The average value over the population first increases up to 3.5 incoming links per node and then falls back to $K = 2$ links per node. As a second example, Figure 5.34 shows the incoming links' evolution for a 5×5-dot pattern classification (see also example 4.6.1). This time, the average value and the value of the best individual are slightly higher (around 2.5 incoming links per node).

These results, though not concluding, are very interesting and suggest that the networks' topology self-organizes towards an average connectivity of $K = 2$ for large networks. Experiments have shown that networks with exactly $K = 2$ incoming links per node behave in a very similar manner than networks with an average connectivity of $K = 2$. Turing was certainly right in choosing networks with two incoming links per node!

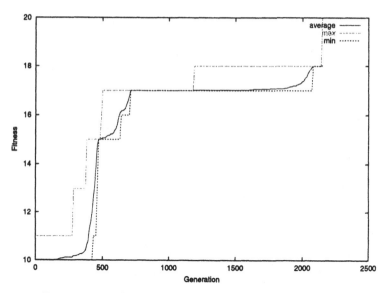

Fig. 5.32. Fitness graph of the 16×16 dot pattern classification by an $N = 1{,}000$-node TB-type network. Each node was allowed to have zero up to N incoming links.

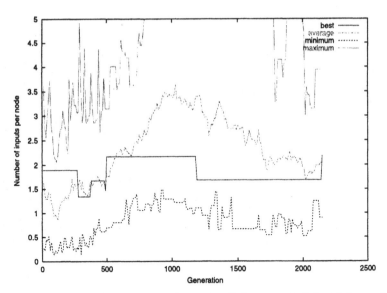

Fig. 5.33. Evolution of the number of incoming links per node (16 × 16-dot pattern classification, 1,000-node network).

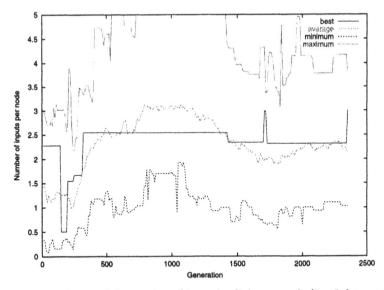

Fig. 5.34. Evolution of the number of incoming links per node (5 × 5-dot pattern classification, 500-node network).

5.11 Hypercomputation: Computing Beyond the Turing Limit with Turing's Neural Networks?

Turing proposed the Turing machine in 1936 [185] (see also Sections 2.1.2 and 2.1.3) as a model of a mathematician that solves an algorithmic problem using paper and pencil. Along with others, including Church, Post, Gödel, Kleene, etc., Turing laid the fundamentals for modern computing science. The Church-Turing thesis (CT thesis) states that a universal Turing machine can carry out *any* effective computation, i.e., it can simulate any other machine capable of performing a well-defined computational procedure. In this context, "effective" is a synonym for "mechanical". There exist many different formulations of the Church-Turing thesis and it has often been misinterpreted. Copeland and Sylvan [41] provide an overview of several typical statements. Trakhtenbrot [179] provides a comparison of the Church and the Turing approaches. Interested readers might also take a look at Hasslacher's paper "Beyond the Turing Machine" [81] and at Galton's paper about the nature of the Church-Turing thesis [68]. He argues that the study of complex, nonlinear, and self-organizing systems might lead to the construction of new kinds of computational models which cannot efficiently be simulated by the traditional concept of a Turing machine.

One of the most accessible formulations of Turing's thesis is probably the following:

> "It is found in practice that LCMs can do anything that could be described as 'rule of thumb' or 'purely mechanical'" [192, p. 7].

The term "LCM" stands for logical computing machine (see also Section 2.1.2).

Modern versions of the Church-Turing thesis often state that no realizable computing device could be more powerful—aside from the speedup—than a universal Turing machine. Even a strong version of the thesis—stating that no realizable physical device can be more powerful than a Turing machine—has not been refuted. Indeed, nobody has found so far a physical computing device that is computationally more powerful than a Turing machine. Even *quantum computing* has been proved by Deutsch in 1985 to be UTM-equivalent only:

> "Every finitely realizable physical system can be perfectly simulated by a universal model computing machine operating by finite means" [51, p. 99].

The Church-Turing thesis has even been (ab)used to formally approach the fuzzy notion of intelligence:

> "What is human computable is computable by a universal Turing machine" [26].

The interested reader is referred to the Stanford Encyclopedia of Philosophy[1] that contains a chapter about the Church-Turing thesis written by Copeland.

But does a universal Turing machine really capture the essence of any and all forms of computing? Or, are there *hypercomputers*, also called *super-Turing machines*, capable of going beyond the Turing limit? Hypercomputation[2] is an emerging field of research and was the focus of a recent workshop in London[3]. Hypercomputation concerns the study of computation beyond the computational capabilities of the Turing machine.

Turing himself presented a model of an abstract hypercomputer—the *O-machine*—in his 1938 doctoral thesis supervised by Church (published in 1939 as a paper [186]). An O-machine is a universal Turing machine augmented by an *oracle* or "black box". The oracle performs a computation which a universal Turing machine operating in finite time cannot compute [40]. Turing used his oracle to describe an abstract mathematical and uncomputable operation. He gave no indication on how such an oracle might be implemented but wrote that:

> "We shall not go any further into the nature of this oracle apart from saying that it cannot be a machine".

Thus, Turing was aware that his O-machines could not be implemented physically! It is important to note that any speculation on building physical hypercomputers—computers that compute the uncomputable—has *no* basis in Turing's writings. This should, however, not prevent researchers from further investigations on possible physical super-Turing machines since neither Church nor Turing had demonstrated the impossibility of hypercomputers.

As already stated above, so far, nobody has found a physical computing device that is computationally more powerful than a Turing machine. There exist, however, many *Gedankenexperiments* in idealized and hypothetical universes that allow the construction of non-physical hypercomputers. One of the best known hypercomputer models has been presented by Hava Siegelmann. The model is based on analog recurrent neural networks (ARNN) [163–165]. An analog recurrent neural network is a finite network of neurons and connections wherein the synaptic weight associated with each connection is a real (analog) value. Siegelmann showed that analog recurrent neural networks are more powerful than the Turing-machine model in that they can perform computations provably uncomputable by a universal Turing machine. When the real synaptic weights are replaced by rational numbers the network's computational power is reduced to that of a Turing machine only.

---

[1] Stanford Encyclopedia of Philosophy: http://plato.stanford.edu.

[2] Hypercomputation research network: http://www.hypercomputation.net. Note that this section is partly based on a yet unpublished paper written together with Moshe Sipper [178].

[3] Hypercomputation Workshop, University College, London, May 24, 2000, http://www.alanturing.net/conference/hyper/hypercom.html.

The *accelerating universal Turing machine (AUTM)* [36, 37, 173] is a hypercomputer that executes the program on its tape at an accelerating rate. The first operation needs one time unit to complete, the second 0.5 time units, the third 0.25 time units, etc. The accelerating universal Turing machine requires a maximum of two time units to execute any possible program. Thus, even a program that does not terminate would be finished in two units only. An accelerating universal Turing machine can compute the infinite in finite time! That's probably the moment one must admit that *Gedankenexperimente* have limited validity only.

Definition 5.11.1 (Execution time of an AUTM)

$$1 + \frac{1}{2} + \frac{1}{4} + \cdots + \frac{1}{2^n} + \cdots = 2 \qquad (5.12)$$

∎

Mike Stannett presented another hypercomputer model—the analogue X-machine—and showed that it can solve the classical *halting problem* that no Turing machine is able to solve [172]. The approach is based on the fact that true analogue systems are computationally more powerful than discrete systems. Just as no universal Turing machine could ever be built since we could not provide an infinite tape, it is very likely that Stannett's analogue machine could never be built.

Concerning Turing's neural networks, Copeland and Proudfoot suggested that:

> "In principle, even a suitable B-type network can compute the uncomputable, provided the activity of the neurons is desynchronized" [40]

This, however, remains to be proved. By definition, an uncomputable function is a function that cannot be computed by any algorithm (equivalently, not by any Turing machine). A Turing neural network is a completely deterministic system and there seems to be no reason why an asynchronous (but deterministic) update of its neurons would allow it to compute beyond the Turing limit. If the neurons are updated completely randomly (not pseudo randomly), the network will no longer compute any function since it evolves nondeterministically and different results will be obtained for one and the same input.

The practicality of physical hypercomputation has, in fact, been questioned by several researchers. Most hypercomputer models involve analog computation with infinite precision or try to compute the infinite in finite time. Given the lessons of quantum mechanics, it seems Nature would not tolerate our building infinitely precise machines. Moreover, the effect of noise on analog computation presents yet another obstacle to the implementation of hypermachines. As for quantum computation—wherein physical phenomena at the quantum level are directly employed to build more powerful computers (at least in theory)—it is too early to tell whether this domain holds any promise where hypercomputation is concerned. This is not to say that quantum computers cannot compute much *faster* than classical ones.

Assume, nonetheless, you have managed to overcome these implementation obstacles and (pseudo-)implement a hypercomputer; to what use could you now put it? Perhaps you could build a "brain": one of the major application domains of hypercomputation being envisaged is that of machine intelligence. This raises the question of whether the human brain itself is a super-Turing machine, an issue over which opinions diverge widely. Most computational brain models presented to date are less powerful than a universal Turing machine. On the other hand, the modest success of classical artificial intelligence has urged researchers such as Mike Stannett to speculate that:

> "[i]f biological systems really do implement analogue or quantum computation, or perhaps some mixture of the two, it is highly likely that they are provably more powerful computationally than Turing machines" [172].

This statement implies that truly intelligent behaviour cannot be implemented on standard digital machines, an opinion shared by Roger Penrose [141, 142] who believes that mechanical intelligence is impossible since purely physical processes are uncomputable. If it turns out that the universe is in fact continuous, then it would seem in fact very unlikely that computational processes tell the full story of how nature works. The interested reader is also referred to Copeland's paper on "Turing's O-machines, Searle, Penrose and the brain" [38].

Turing himself believed that the brain should be considered as a discrete state machine. In his *Mind* paper he wrote:

> "The nervous system is certainly not a discrete-state machine. A small error in the information about the size of a nervous impulse impinging on a neuron, may make a large difference to the size of the outgoing impulse. It may be argued that, this being so, one cannot expect to be able to mimic the behavior of the nervous system with a discrete-state machine" [188, p. 451].

Turing was aware that the physical processes in the brain are analogue, but believed that the features of the brain relevant to thinking or intelligence can be mimicked by a discrete-state machine. In the *Mind* paper, he then briefly explains how a digital machine can mimic the behaviour of an analogue machine.

A Turing machine is a closed system that does not accept input while operating, whereas the brain continually receives input from the environment. Wegner wrote:

"The claim that interactive systems have richer behavior than algorithms is surprisingly easy to prove. Turing machines cannot model interaction machines (which extend Turing machines with interactive input/output) because interaction is not expressible by a finite initial input string" [211].

Copeland and Sylvan have proposed the *coupled Turing machine* which is connected to the environment via one or more input channels [41]. However, any coupled machine with a finite input stream can be simulated by a universal Turing machine since the data can be written on the machine's tape before it begins operation (note that a machine with a finite lifespan handles a finite amount of input data). Consider the following *Gedankenexperiment*: we've managed to record all of a human's inputs and outputs, received and emitted over a lifetime of interaction; would a universal Turing machine or a Turing neural network now be able to map the inputs to the outputs? In other words, can a human's lifelong behaviour be described by a Turing-machine computable function? Copeland wrote:

"[...] it would—or should—be one of the great astonishments of science if the activity of Mother Nature were never to stray beyond the bounds of Turing-machine computability" [41].

We have seen in Section 5.2 that Turing's neural networks are universal computers, i.e., that they can compute anything that a Turing machine can compute. So far, no speculation on super-Turing capabilities of Turing's neural networks has lead to something useful. Thus, the answer to this section is straightforward: to date, neither Turing's neural networks nor any other physical device was able to compute beyond the Turing machine limit.

6. Epilogue

> *Dum loquimur, fugerit invida*
> *Aetas: carpe diem, quam minimum credula postero.*
> *While we're talking, envious time is fleeing: seize the day, put no trust in*
> *the future.*
> — Horace, *Odes*, 65–8 BC.

It is time now for some concluding remarks. During all the time I was absorbed with Turing's fascinating ideas, I got comments and feedback from many people all over the world. As always, there were useful and useless, positive and negative comments. One of the most frequent questions asked was probably the following (or very similar):

"What are these nets good for?"

This is obviously an unsophisticated question that might be asked of any topic. The comment of an anonymous reviewer of a paper submitted to a well-known international conference about neural network models gets down to brass tacks:

"It is all a very nice read but ultimately is not very useful to anyone except to perhaps persuade them that this is a dead end, sorry...".

So much for the rather discerning feedback. The question of "boolean or not" is certainly still an open one. As already mentioned in the introduction, many a researcher is still convinced that the essential functions of the brain could be mimicked by boolean models. One of the counter-examples is the computer scientist and author of *Artificial Minds*, Stan Franklin. He states:

"Mind is best viewed as continues, as opposed to Boolean. It's more useful to allow degrees of mind than demand either mind or no mind" [61].

It would certainly be one of the great astonishments of science if the fundamental activity of the human brain could be modeled by a purely boolean and synchronous model. For many physical and biological phenomena, the assumption of asynchrony seems more plausible. Thus, Turing's connectionism was, from today's point of view, certainly much too simple. However, that does not derogate his fascinating ideas for that time.

Today, there certainly exist much more powerful neural models and it would be completely useless to compare present pattern classification systems with a system based on Turing's simple NAND gates. Recent work of Igor Aleksander emphasized the advantage of weightless systems for optimal hardware implementations [4]. Apart from the fact that Turing's unorganized machines can also very efficiently be implemented in hardware (allowing at the same time to implement very large networks because of the simplicity of the neurons), I do not see any real-world killer application for them.

As the work of Stuart Kauffman and others showed, random boolean networks are of a great interest for the study of self-organizing phenomenon, complex dynamics, chaotic behaviour, etc. There exist many complex systems of interacting elements (e.g., *gene regulatory networks*, etc.) that can be investigated by means of boolean networks. The complex dynamics of Turing's neural networks is a fascinating domain with many open questions. Why do $K = 2$ random boolean networks offer the most interesting behaviour? Why do the networks self-organize towards a critical interconnectivity of $K = 2$ incoming connections per node? Many books have been written on the beautiful, amazing and complex dynamical systems, however, many phenomena still remain unexplained.

The work conducted this far is mainly of historical interest and investigated the foundations of today's connectionism. It finished off some of Turing's thoughts and thus, for example, his dream of applying some sort of "genetical search" to organize the unorganized machines has become reality. Furthermore, the investigation of his networks from the the complex-systems-theory point of view made a bridge between his connectionist ideas and his work on morphogenesis.

Today, we are still far away from the creation of artificial human-like intelligence. Mankind has certainly constructed extremely impressive computing systems and extremely large and complex networks that perform operations that no human brain could ever complete. But are these systems really intelligent? Intelligence does unfortunately not spontaneously emerge with growing computational power (at least so far). All "intelligent" systems constructed so far (e.g., *Deep Blue*, Hugo de Garis *CAM-brain*, etc.) remain in the domain of algorithms and thus in the computational domain of Turing machines. Will a revolutionary hypercomputational model rescue us? Or is computational intelligence doomed to eternal failure?

We have entered a new millennium. There will be time for new ideas.

Useful Web-Sites

- Book web-site:

  http://www.teuscher.ch/turing

- Andrew Hodges' Turing web-site:

  http://www.turing.org.uk

- "The Turing Archive for the History of Computing", University of Canterbury, New Zealand:

  http://www.alanturing.net

- "The Turing Digital Archive". Contains many original typescripts, letters, and photos:

  http://www.turingarchive.org

- Online version of Turing's "MIND" paper "Computing Machinery and Intelligence":

  http://www.abelard.org/turpap/turpap.htm

- Craig Webster's web-site about Turing's neural networks:

  http://home.clear.net.nz/pages/cw

- Hypercomputation research network:

  http://www.hypercomputation.net

- Stanford Encyclopedia of Philosophy:

> http://plato.stanford.edu

- Neural Network FAQs:

> ftp://ftp.sas.com/pub/neural/FAQ.html

- Brain/Mind Resources:

> http://mind.phil.vt.edu/www/mind.html

- Some Turing Machine Simulators:

> http://www.igs.net/ tril/tm/tm.html

> http://www.turing.org.uk/turing/scrapbook/tmjava.html

> http://www.bvu.edu/faculty/schweller/Turing.html

List of Figures

List of Tables

List of Examples, Theorems, Definitions, Propositions, and Corollaries

Bibliography

1. NPL Executive Committee Minutes, 20 April 1948, page 7.
2. NPL Executive Committee Minutes, 28 September 1948, page 4.
3. I. Aleksander. Random logic nets: Stability and adaptation. *International Journal of Man-Machine Studies*, 5:115–131, 1973.
4. I. Aleksander. From Wisard to Magnus: A family of weightless virtual neural machines. In Austin [15].
5. I. Aleksander and H. Morton. *An Introduction to Neural Computing*. International Thomson Computer Press, London, UK; Boston, MA, second edition, 1995.
6. I. Aleksander, W. V. Thomas, and P. A. Bowden. WISARD: A radical step foward in image recognition. *Sensor Review*, 4:120–124, July 1984.
7. J. T. Allanson. Some properties of randomly connected neural nets. In C. Cherry, editor. *Proceedings of the 3rd London Symposium on Information Theory*, pages 303–313, Butterworths, London, 1956.
8. S. I. Amari. Characteristics of randomly connected threshold-element networks and network systems. *Proceedings of the IEEE*, 59(1):35–47, January 1971.
9. S. I. Amari. Learning patterns and patterns sequences by self-organizing nets of threshold elements. *IEEE Transactions on Computers*, C-21(11):1197–1206, November 1972.
10. M. A. Arbib, editor. *The Handbook of Brain Theory and Neural Networks*. MIT Press, Cambridge, MA, 1995.
11. W. R. Asbhy. *An Introduction to Cybernetics*. Chapman and Hall, London, 1956.
12. W. R. Asbhy, H. von Forster, and C. C. Walker. Instability of pulse activity in a net with threshold. *Nature*, 196:561, 1966.
13. W. R. Ashby. *Design for a Brain*. Wiley, New York, 1956.
14. P. J. Ashenden. *The Designer's Guide to VHDL*. Morgan Kaufmann Publishers, Inc., San Francisco, CA, 1996.
15. J. Austin, editor. *RAM-Based Neural Networks*, volume 9 of *Progress in Neural Processing*. World Scientific, February 1998.
16. T. Bäck. *Evolutionary Algorithms in Theory and Practice: Evolution Strategies, Evolutionary Programming, Genetic Algorithms*. Oxford University Press, New York, 1996.
17. S. L. Bade and B. L. Hutchings. FPGA-based stochastic neural networks implementation. In *IEEE Workshop on FPGAs for Custom Computing Machines*, pages 189–198, Los Alamitos, CA, April 1994. IEEE Computer Society Press.
18. P. Bak. *How Nature Works: The Science of Self-Organized Criticality*. Springer-Verlag Telos, 1999.
19. P. Bak and L. Chen. Self-organized criticality. *Scientific American*, 265:26–33, January 1991.

20. W. Banzhaf, P. Nordin, R. E. Keller, and F. D. Francone. *Genetic Programming-An Introduction: On the Automatic Evolution of Computer Programs and its Applications.* Morgan Kaufmann Publishers, San Francisco, CA, 1997.

21. D. Bayley, 1997. In interview with B. J. Copeland.

22. E. R. Berlekamp, J. H. Conway, and R. K. Guy. *Winning Ways for your Mathematical Plays,* volume 2: Games in Particular. Academic Press, London, 1982.

23. E. J. W. Boers and H. Kuiper. Biological Metaphors and the Design of Modular Artificial Neural Networks. Master's thesis, Rijksunversität te Leiden, 1992.

24. S. Bornholdt and T. Rohlf. Topological evolution of dynamical networks: Global criticality from local dynamics. *Physical Review Letters,* 84(26):6114–6117, June 2000.

25. J. L. Britton, editor. *Collected Works of A. M. Turing: Pure Mathematics.* North-Holland, Amsterdam, 1992.

26. C. Calude and G. Paun. *Computing with Cells and Atoms: An Introduction to Quantum, DNA and Membrane Computing.* Taylor & Francis, New York, 2000.

27. W. H. Calvin. The Emergence of Intelligence. *Scientific American: Exploring Intelligence,* 9(4):44–50, 1998.

28. P. Carnevali and S. Patarnello. Exhaustive thermodynamical analysis of boolean learning networks. *Europhysics Letters,* 4(10):1199–1204, November 1987.

29. B. E. Carpenter and R. W. Doran, editors. *A. M. Turing's ACE Report of 1946 and Other Papers.* MIT Press, Cambridge, MA, 1986.

30. P. S. Churchland and T. J. Sejnowski. *The Computational Brain.* MIT Press, Cambridge, MA, 1992.

31. A. Clark and P. Millican, editors. *The Legacy of Alan Turing: Connectionism, Concepts, and Folk Psychology,* volume 2. Oxford University Press Inc., New York, 1996.

32. W. A. Clark and B. G. Farley. Generalisation of pattern recognition in a self-organising system. In *Proceedings of the Western Joint Computer Conference,* pages 86–91, 1955.

33. D. J. Comer. *Digital Logic and State Machine Design.* Saunders College Publishing, Fort Worth, TX, third edition, 1995.

34. M. Compiani. Remarks on the paradigms of connectionism. In Clark and Millican [31], chapter 2, pages 45–66.

35. P. A. Cook. *Nonlinear Dynamical Systems.* Prentice-Hall International, London, 1986.

36. B. J. Copeland. Even Turing machines can compute uncomputable functions. In C. Calude, J. Casti, and M. Dinneen, editors. *Unconventional Models of Computation,* pages 150–164. Springer-Verlag, London, 1998.

37. B. J. Copeland. Super Turing-machines. *Complexity,* 4(1):30–32, 1998.

38. B. J. Copeland. Turing's O-machines, Penrose, Searle, and the brain. *Analysis,* 58:128–138, 1998.

39. B. J. Copeland and D. Proudfoot. On Alan Turing's anticipation of connectionism. *Synthese: An International Journal for Epistemology, Methodology and Philosophy of Science,* 108:361–377, 1996. Kluwer Academic Publishers.

40. B. J. Copeland and D. Proudfoot. Alan Turing's forgotten ideas in computer science. *Scientific American,* 280(4):77–81, April 1999.

41. B. J. Copeland and R. Sylvan. Beyond the universal Turing machine. *Australasian Journal of Philosophy,* 77:46–66, 1999.

42. C. Darwin. *The Origin of Species.* John Murray, London, 1859.

43. C. Darwin, 13 August 1946. Letter to Sir Edward Appleton.

44. C. Darwin, 23 July 1947. Letter to Sir Edward Appleton.
45. C. Darwin, 11 November 1947. Letter to A. M. Turing.
46. M. Davis, editor. *The Undecidable.* Raven Press, Hewlett, New York, 1965.
47. M. Davis. *The Universal Computer.* W. W. Norton, 2000.
48. H. de Garis. *Genetic Programming: GenNets, Artificial Nervous Systems, Artificial Embryos.* PhD thesis, Brussels University, 1992.
49. C. Van den Broeck and R. Kawai. Learning in feedforward boolean networks. *Physical Review A,* 42(10):6210–6218, November 1990.
50. B. Derrida and Y. Pomeau. Random networks of automata: A simple annealed approximation. *Europhysics Letters,* 1(2):45–49, 1986.
51. D. Deutsch. Quantum theory, the Church-Turing principle of the Universal Quantum Computer. *Proceedings of the Royal Society of London,* A400:97–117, 1985.
52. R. O. Duda, D. G. Stork, and P. E. Hart. *Pattern Classification.* John Wiley and Sons, second edition, 2000.
53. J. L. Elman. Finding structure in time. *Cognitive Science,* 14:179–211, 1990.
54. J. L. Elman, E. A. Bates, M. H. Johnson, A. Karmiloff-Smith, D. Parisi, and K. Plunkett. *Rethinking Innateness, A Connectionist Perspective on Development.* A Bradford Book, MIT Press, Cambridge, MA; London, UK, 1996.
55. C. R. Evans and A. D. J. Robertson, editors. *Cybernetics: Key Papers.* University Park Press, Baltimore Md. and Manchester, London, 1968.
56. B. G. Farley and W. A. Clark. Simulation of self-organising systems by digital computer. *Institute of Radio Engineers Transactions on Information Theory,* 4:76–84, 1954.
57. G. W. Flake. *The Computational Beauty of Nature. Computer Explorations of Fractals, Chaos, Complex Systems, and Adaptation.* MIT Press, Cambridge, MA, 1998.
58. T. Flowers, 1998. In interview with B. J. Copeland.
59. R. W. Floyd and R. Beigel. *The Language of Machines: An Introduction to Computability and Formal Languages.* Computer Science Press, New York, 1994.
60. D. B. Fogel. *Evolutionary Computation: Toward a New Philosophy of Machine Intelligence.* IEEE Press, Piscataway, NJ, second edition, 1999.
61. S. Franklin. *Artificial Minds: An Exploration of the Mechanisms of Mind.* MIT Press, Cambridge, MA, 1995.
62. S. Franklin and M. Garzon. Neural Computability. *Progress in Neural Networks,* 1 (edited by O. M. Omidvar):128–144, 1990. Ablex, Norwood, NJ.
63. W. J. Freeman. Role of chaotic dynamics in neural plasticity. In van Pelt et al. [199], chapter 21, page 319.
64. K. Fukushima. Cognitron: A self-organizing multilayered neural network model. *Biological Cybernetics,* 20:121–136, 1965.
65. K. Fukushima, S. Miyake, and T. Ito. Neocognitron: A neural network model for a mechanism of visual pattern recognition. *IEEE Transactions on Systems, Man, and Cybernetics,* 13:826–834, 1983.
66. K. Fukushima and N. Wake. Handwitten alphanumeric character recognition by the Neocognitron. *IEEE Transactions on Neural Networks,* 2(3):355–365, 1991.
67. K. Furukawa, D. Michie, and S. Muggleton, editors. *Machine Intelligence 15.* Oxford University Press, New York, 1999.
68. A. Galton. The Church-Turing thesis: Its nature and status. In Millican and Clark [124], chapter 8, pages 137–164.
69. R. Gandy. Letter to M. Newman, undated, but marked 'Automn 1954'.
70. R. Gandy, 1995. In interview with B. J. Copeland.

71. R. Gandy. Human versus mechanical intelligence. In Millican and Clark [124], chapter 7, pages 125–136.

72. H. Gardner. A Multiplicity of Intelligences. *Scientific American: Exploring Intelligence*, 9(4):19–23, 1998.

73. M. Gardner. Mathematical games: The fantastic combinations of John Conway's new solitaire game 'Life'. *Scientific American*, 232(4):120–124, October 1970.

74. L. Glass. Chaos in neural systems. In Arbib [10], pages 186–189.

75. A. L. Goldberger, D. R. Rigney, and B. J. West. Fractals and chaos in human psychology. *Scientific American*, pages 43–49, February 1990.

76. R. O. Grondin, W. Porod, C. M. Loeffler, and D. K. Ferry. Synchronous and asynchronous systems of threshold elements. *Biological Cybernetics*, 49:1–7, 1983.

77. F. Gruau. *Neural Network Synthesis Using Cellular Encoding and the Genetic Algorithm*. PhD thesis, PhD Thesis, Ecole Normale Supérieure de Lyon, 1994.

78. M. R. Guevara, L. Glass, M. C. Mackey, and A. Shrier. Chaos in neurobiology. *IEEE Transactions on Man, Systems and Cybernetics*, 13(5):790–798, 1983.

79. P. J. B. Hancock. *Coding Strategies for Genetic Algorithms and Neural Nets*. PhD thesis, Department of Computing Science and Mathematics, University of Stirling, 1992.

80. I. Harvey and T. Bossomaier. Time out of joint: Attractors in asynchronous random boolean networks. In P. Husbands and I. Harvey, editors. *Proceedings of the Fourth European Conference on Artificial Life*, pages 67–75. MIT Press, Cambridge, MA, 1997.

81. B. Hasslacher. Beyond the Turing machine. In Herken [86], pages 387–402.

82. M. H. Hassoun. *Fundamentals of Artificial Neural Networks*. A Bradford Book, MIT Press, Cambridge, MA; London, UK, 1995.

83. G. Hayes, November 1979. Communication to Michael Woodger.

84. S. Haykin. *Neural Networks: A Comprehensive Foundation*. Prentice Hall, New Jersey, second edition, 1999.

85. D. Hebb. *The Organization of Behavior*. John Wiley, New York, 1949.

86. R. Herken, editor. *The Universal Turing Machine: A Half-Century Survey*. Springer-Verlag, Wien, second edition, 1995.

87. J. Hertz. Computing with attractors. In Arbib [10], pages 230–234.

88. D. W. Hillis. *The Connection Machine*. MIT Press, Cambridge, MA; London, UK, 1985.

89. A. Hodges. Alan Turing and the Turing machine. In Herken [86], pages 3–14.

90. A. Hodges. *Turing: A Natural Philosopher*. The Great Philosophers Series. Routledge, New York, 1999.

91. A. Hodges. *Alan Turing: The Enigma*. Walker & Company, New York, 2000.

92. Andrew Hodges. *Turing: A Natural Philosopher*. Phoenix Press, London, 1997.

93. J. H. Holland. *Adaption in Natural and Artificial Systems*. The University of Michigan Press, Ann Arbor, MI, 1975.

94. J. R. Hurford. Random boolean nets and features of language. *IEEE Transactions on Evolutionary Computation*, 5(2):111–116, April 2001.

95. D. C. Ince, editor. *Collected Works of A. M. Turing: Mechanical Intelligence*. North-Holland, Amsterdam, 1992.

96. J. S. Judd. Learning in neural networks is hard. In M. Caudill and C. Butler, editors. *First IEEE International Conference on Neural Networks*, volume 2, pages 685–692, San Diego, 1987. IEEE, New York.

97. J. S. Judd. *Neural Network Design and the Complexity of Learning*. A Pradford Book, MIT Press, Cambridge, MA, 1990.

98. S. A. Kauffman. Metabolic stability and epigenesis in randomly connected genetic nets. *Journal of Theoretical Biology*, 22:437–467, 1968.

99. S. A. Kauffman. *The Origins of Order: Self-Organization and Selection in Evolution*. Oxford University Press, New York; Oxford, 1993.

100. S. A. Kauffman. *At Home in the Universe*. Oxford University Press, New York; Oxford, 1995.

101. S. A. Kauffman. *Investigations*. Oxford University Press, New York; Oxford, 2000.

102. H. Kitano. Designing Neural Networks using Genetic Algorithms with Graph Generation System. *Complex Systems*, 4:461–476, 1990.

103. S. C. Kleene. Reflections on Church's thesis. *Notre Dame Journal of Formal Logic*, 28:490–498, 1987.

104. Z. Kohavi. *Switching and Finite Automata Theory*. McGraw-Hill, New York, second edition, 1978.

105. M. Korkin, N. E. Nawa, and D. de Garis. A "spike interval information coding" representation of ATR's CAM-brain machine (CBM). In M. Sipper, D. Mange, and A. Pérez-Uribe, editors. *Proceedings of the Second International Conference on Evolvable Systems (ICES'98)*, Lecture Notes in Computer Science, No 1478, pages 256–267, Lausanne, Switzerland, September 1998. Springer-Verlag, Berlin, Germany.

106. J. R. Koza. *Genetic Programming: On the Programming of Computers by Means of Natural Selection*. MIT Press, Cambridge, MA, 1992.

107. J. R. Koza, F. H. Bennett III, D. Andre, and M. A. Keane. *Genetic Programming III: Darwinian Invention and Problem Solving*. Morgan Kaufmann, San Francisco, CA, 1999.

108. S. Krikpatrick, C. D. Gelatt Jr., and M. P. Vecchi. Optimization by simulated annealing. *Science*, 220:671–680, 1983.

109. R. Kurzweil. *The Age of Spiritual Machines: When Computers Exceed Human Intelligence*. Viking, 1999.

110. C. Langton, editor. *Artificial Life. Proceedings of the Interdisciplinary Workshop on the Synthesis and Simulation of Living Systems*, Redwood City, CA, 1989. Addison-Wesley.

111. C. G. Langton. Computation at the edge of chaos: Phase transition and emergent computation. *Physica D*, 42:12–37, 1990.

112. A. Lindenmayer. Mathematical Models for Cellular Interaction in Development, Parts I and II. *Journal of Theoretical Biology*, 18:280–315, 1968.

113. D. Mange and M. Tomassini, editors. *Bio-Inspired Computing Machines: Towards Novel Computational Architectures*. Presses Polytechniques et Universitaires Romandes, Lausanne, Switzerland, 1998.

114. D. Martland. Auto-associative pattern storage using synchronous boolean networks. In *Proceedings of the First IEEE International Conference on Neural Networks*, volume III, pages 355–366, San Diego, CA, 1987.

115. D. Martland. Behaviour of autonomous, (synchronous), boolean networks. In *Proceedings of the First IEEE International Conference on Neural Networks*, volume II, pages 243–250, San Diego, CA, 1987.

116. D. Martland. Configurable boolean networks. In L. Personnaz and G. Dreyfus, editors. *Neural Networks from Models to Applications. Proceedings of the First European Conference on Neural Networks, nEuro'88*, volume III, pages 355–366, IDSET, Paris, June 1988.

117. D. Martland. Dynamic behavior of boolean networks. In I. Aleksander, editor. *Neural Computing Architectures: The Design of Brain-Like Machines*, chapter 11, pages 217–235. North Oxford Academic, London, 1989.

118. E. Mayoraz. *Feedforward Boolean Neural Networks with Discrete Weights: Computational Power and Training.* PhD thesis, Swiss Federal Institute of Technology Lausanne (EPFL), CH–1015 Lausanne, 1993. Thesis No 1157.

119. W. S. McCulloch and W. H. Pitts. A logical calculus of the ideas immanent in neural nets. *Bulletin of Mathematical Biophysics*, 5:115–133, 1943.

120. Z. Michalewicz. *Genetic Algorithms + Data Structures = Evolution Programs.* Springer-Verlag, Heidelberg, third edition, 1996.

121. D. Michie. In interviews with B. J. Copeland, 1995, 1998.

122. D. Michie. Unpublished note.

123. D. F. Miller, P. M. Todd, and S. U. Hegde. Designing Neural Networks using Genetic Algorithms. In J. D. Schaffer, editor. *Third International Conference on Genetic Algorithms*, pages 379–384. Morgan Kaufmann, 1989.

124. P. Millican and A. Clark, editors. *The Legacy of Alan Turing: Machines and Thought*, volume 1. Oxford University Press Inc., New York, 1996.

125. M. L. Minsky. *Computation: Finite and Infinite Machines.* Prentice-Hall, Englewood Cliffs, NJ, 1967.

126. M. L. Minsky and S. Papert. *Perceptron: An Introduction to Computational Geometry.* MIT Press, Cambridge, MA, 1972.

127. M. Mitchell. *An Introduction to Genetic Algorithms.* MIT Press, Cambridge, MA, 1996.

128. M. Newman, 22 December 1948. Letter to D. Brunt.

129. J. Niittylahti. Hardware implementation of boolean neural network using simulated annealing. Master's thesis, Tampere University of Technology, Tampere, Finland, 1992.

130. J. Niittylahti. *Boolean Neural Network Implementations.* PhD thesis, Tampere University of Technology, Tampere, Finland, 1995.

131. J. Niittylahti. Hardware prototypes of a boolean neural network and the simulated annealing optimization method. *International Journal of Neural Systems*, 7(1):45–52, March 1996.

132. J. Niittylahti. Boolean neural network trained with simulated annealing. In O. M. Omidvar, editor. *Progress in Neural Networks*, volume 6. Intellect Ltd, London, 1999.

133. S. Nolfi and D. Floreano. Learning and evolution. *Autonomous Robots*, 7(1):89–113, 1999.

134. S. Nolfi and D. Floreano. *Evolutionary Robotics: The Biology, Intelligence, and Technology of Self-Organizing Machines.* MIT Press, Cambridge, MA, 2000.

135. S. Nolfi and D. Parisi. Growing neural networks. Technical Report PCIA-91-15, Institute of Psychology, CNR, Rome, 1991. Also in Proceedings of ALIFE III, 1992.

136. R. C. O'Reilly and Y. Munakata. *Computational Explorations in Cognitive Neuroscience.* A Bradford Book, MIT Press, Cambridge, MA, 2000.

137. E. A. Di Paolo. Searching for rhythms in asynchronous boolean networks. In M. A. Bedau, J. S. McCaskill, N. H. Packard, and S. Rassmussen, editors. *Proceedings of the Seventh International Conference on Artificial Life*, Reed College, Portland, OR, August 1–6 2000. A Bradford Book, MIT Press, Cambridge, MA; London, UK.

138. E. A. Di Paolo. Rhythmic and non-rhythmic attractors in asynchronous random boolean networks. *BioSystems*, 59(3):185–195, 2001.

139. A. Patarnello and P. Carnevali. Learning networks of neurons with boolean logic. *Europhysics Letters*, 4(4):503–508, August 1987.

140. S. Patarnello and P. Carnevali. Learning capabilities of boolean networks. In I. Aleksander, editor. *Neural Computing Architectures: The Design of Brain-Like Machines*, chapter 7, pages 117–129. North Oxford Academic, London, 1989.

141. R. Penrose. *The Emperor's New Mind*. Oxford University Press, 1989.

142. R. Penrose. *Shadows of the Mind*. Vintage, 1995.

143. J. B. Pollack. *On Connectionist Models of Neural Language Processing*. PhD thesis, Computer Science Department, University of Illinois, Urbana, IL, 1987. (Available as MCCS-87-100, Computing Research Laboratory, NMSU, Las Cruces, NM).

144. P. Prusinkiewicz and A. Lindenmayer. *The Algorithmic Beauty of Plants*. Springer-Verlag, New York, 1990.

145. F. Radley, 1 November 1946. Letter to Sir Charles Darwin.

146. B. Randell, editor. *The Origins of Digital Computers*. Springer-Verlag, Berlin, 1982.

147. H. F. Restrepo, D. Mange, and M. Sipper. A self-replicating universal Turing machine: From von Neumann's dream to new embryonic circuits. In M. A. Bedau, J. S. McCaskill, N. H. Packard, and S. Rassmussen, editors. *Proceedings of the Seventh International Conference on Artificial Life*, pages 3–12, Reed College, Portland, OR, August 1–6 2000. A Bradford Book, MIT Press, Cambridge, MA; London, UK.

148. F. Rieke, D. Warland, R. de R. van Steveninck, and W. Bialek. *Spikes: Exploring the Neural Code*. A Bradford Book, MIT Press, Cambridge, MA; London, UK, second edition, 1996.

149. S. Roberts and S. Turega. Evolving neural networks structures: An evaluation of encoding techniques. In D. W. Pearson, N. C. Steele, and R. F. Albrecht, editors. *Artificial Neural Nets and Genetic Algorithms. Proceedings of the International Conference on Artificial Neural Networks and Genetic Algorithms, ICANNGA'95*, Wien, 1995. Springer-Verlag.

150. R. Rojas. *Neural Networks: A Systematic Introduction*. Springer-Verlag, Berlin, 1996.

151. F. Rosenblatt. The perceptron, a perceiving and recognizing automaton. *Cornell Aeronautical Laboratory Report No. 85-460-1*, 1957.

152. F. Rosenblatt. The perceptron: A probabilistic model for information storage and organization in the brain. *Psychological Review*, 65:386–408, 1958.

153. F. Rosenblatt. *Principles of Neurodynamics*. Spartan, Washington, DC, 1961.

154. L. I. Rozonoér. Random logical nets I. *Automation and Remote Control*, 5:773–781, 1969. Translation of Avtomatika i Telemekhanika.

155. J. G. Rueckl, K. R. Cave, and S. M. Kosslyn. Why are 'what' and 'where' processed by separate cortical visual systems? A computational investigation. *Journal of Cognitive Neuroscience*, 1:171–186, 1989.

156. D. E. Rumelhart and J. L. McClelland. *Parallel Distributed Processing*, volume 1: Foundations. MIT Press, Cambridge, MA, 1986.

157. E. Sanchez, M. Sipper, J. O. Haenni, J. L. Beuchat, A. Stauffer, and A. Pérez-Uribe. Static and Dynamic Configurable Systems. *IEEE Transactions on Computers*, 48(6):556–564, June 1999.

158. P. T. Saunders, editor. *Collected Works of A. M. Turing: Morphogenesis*. North-Holland, Amsterdam, 1992.

159. J. R. Searle. *The Rediscovery of the Mind*. MIT Press, Cambridge, MA, 1992.

160. O. G. Selfridge. "Pandemonium": A paradigm for learning. In *Mechanisation of Thought Processes: Proceedings of a Symposium held at the National Physical Laboratory*, pages 513–526, 1958.

161. O. G. Selfridge and U. Neisser. Pattern recognition by machine. *Scientific American*, 203(2):60–68, 1960.
162. C. Shannon and J. Feldman. *Automata Studies*. Princeton University Press, Princeton, NJ, 1956.
163. H. T. Siegelmann. Computation beyond the Turing limit. *Science*, 268:545–548, April 1995.
164. H. T. Siegelmann. The simple dynamics of super Turing theories. *Theoretical Computer Science*, 168:461–472, 1996.
165. H. T. Siegelmann. *Neural Networks and Analog Computation: Beyond the Turing Limit*. Progress in Theoretical Computer Science. Birkhauser Verlag, November 1998.
166. H. T. Siegelmann and E. D. Sontag. Turing computability with neural networks. *Applied Mathematics Letter*, 4(6):77–80, 1991.
167. H. T. Siegelmann and E. D. Sontag. On the computational power of neural nets. In *Proceedings of the 5th Annual ACM Workshop on Computational Learning Theory*, pages 440–449, 1992.
168. H. A. Simon. Machine as mind. In Millican and Clark [124], chapter 5, pages 81–102.
169. C. A. Skarda and W. J. Freeman. How brains make chaos in order to make sense of the world. *Behavioral Brain Science*, 10(161–195), 1987.
170. D. R. Smith and C. H. Davidson. Maintained activity in neural nets. *Journal of the ACM*, 9:268–279, 1962.
171. E. D. Sontag. Automata and neural networks. In Arbib [10].
172. M. Stannett. X-machines and the halting problem: Building a super-Turing machine. *Formal Aspects of Computing*, 2:331–341, 1990.
173. I. Stewart. Deciding the undecidable. *Nature*, 352:664–665, 1991.
174. R. S. Sutton and A. G. Barto. *Reinforcement Learning: An Introduction*. A Bradford Book, MIT Press, Cambride, MA, 1998.
175. A. H. Taub, editor. *Collected Works of John von Neumann*, volume 5. Pergamon Press, Oxford, 1961.
176. C. Teuscher. A simple MATLAB toolbox for Turing neural networks. http://www.teuscher.ch/turing.
177. C. Teuscher. Study, implementation, and evolution of the artificial neural networks proposed by Alan M. Turing. A revival of his "schoolboy" ideas. Master's thesis, Swiss Federal Institute of Technology Lausanne, Logic Systems Laboratory, EPFL-DI-LSL, CH-1015 Lausanne, February 2000.
178. C. Teuscher and M. Sipper. Hypercomputation: Hype or computation? *Communications of the ACM*, 2001. (To appear).
179. B. A. Trakhtenbrot. Comparing the Church and Turing approaches: Two prophetical messages. In Herken [86], pages 557–582.
180. S. M. Trimberger. *Field-Programmable Gate Array Technology*. Kluwer Academic Publishers, Boston, 1994.
181. Andrew Hodges' Turing Web-Site. http://www.turing.org.uk.
182. The Turing Archive for the History of Computing. University of Canterbury, New Zealand. http://www.alanturing.net.
183. A. M. Turing. Letter to Woodger, undated, received 12 February 1951.
184. A. M. Turing. Letter to W. Ross Ashby. A digital facsimile may be viewed in "The Turing Archive for the History of Computing": http://www.alanturing.net/turing_asbhy. The undated letter was probably written in 1946 and certainly prior to October 1947.

185. A. M. Turing. On computable numbers with an application to the Entschei-dungsproblem. In *Proceedings of the London Mathematical Society*, volume 42 of *2*, pages 230–265, 1936-7. Corrections in *Proceedings of the London Mathematical Society*, volume 43, pages 544–546, 1937.

186. A. M. Turing. Systems of logic based on ordinals. In *Proceedings of the London Mathematical Society*, volume 45 of *2*, pages 161–228, 1939. This was also Turing's Princeton Ph.D. thesis (1938).

187. A. M. Turing. Lecture to the London Mathematical Society. In Carpenter and Doran [29].

188. A. M. Turing. Computing machinery and intelligence. *Mind*, 59(236):433–460, 1950.

189. A. M. Turing. The world problem in semi-groups with cancellation. *Annals of Mathematics*, 52:491–505, 1950.

190. A. M. Turing, 8 February 1951. Letter to J. Z. Young.

191. A. M. Turing. The chemical basis of morphogenesis. *Philosophical Transactions of the Royal Society of London*, B 237:37–72, 1952.

192. A. M. Turing. Intelligent machinery. In B. Meltzer and D. Michie, editors. *Machine Intelligence*, volume 5, pages 3–23. Edinburgh University Press, Edinburgh, 1969.

193. A. M. Turing. Proposal for development in the mathematics division of an Automatic Computing Engine (ACE). In Carpenter and Doran [29].

194. A. M. Turing. Computing machinery and intelligence. In Ince [95], pages 133–160.

195. A. M. Turing. Intelligent machinery. In Ince [95], pages 107–127.

196. A. M. Turing. A lecture and two radio broadcasts by Alan Turing (edited by B. J. Copeland). In Furukawa et al. [67], pages 445–475.

197. A. M. Turing. The Turing-Wilkinson lectures on the Automatic Computing Engine (edited by B. J. Copeland). In Furukawa et al. [67], pages 381–444.

198. J. Vaario, S. Ohsuga, and K. Hori. Connectionist Modeling Using Lindenmayer Systems. In *Information Modeling and Knowledge Bases: Foundations, Theory, and Applications*, volume 10, pages 496–510. Frontiers in artificial intelligence and applications, 1991.

199. J. van Pelt, M. A. Corner, H. B. M. Uylings, and F. H. Lopes da Silva, editors. *The Self-Organizing Brain: From Growth Cones to Functional Networks*, volume 102 of *Progress in Brain Research*. Elsevier Science BV, 1994.

200. M. von Daalen, P. Jeavons, and J. Shawe-Taylor. A stochastic neural architecture that exploits dynamically reconfigurable FPGAs. In *Proceedings of the IEEE Workshop on FPGA for Custom Computing Machines*, pages 202–211, 1993.

201. Ch. von der Malsburg. Self-Organization and the Brain. In Arbib [10].

202. J. von Neumann. First draft of a report on the EDVAC. Moore School of Electrical Engineering, University of Pennsylvania, PA. In Randell [146], pages 383–392.

203. J. von Neumann. Probabilistic logic and the synthesis of reliable organisms from unreliable components. In *Automata Studies* [162], pages 43–98.

204. J. von Neumann. The NORC and problems in high speed computing. In Taub [175], pages 238–247.

205. M. D. Vose. *The Simple Genetic Algorithm: Foundations and Theory*. MIT Press, Cambridge, MA, 1999.

206. J. F. Wakerly. *Digital Design: Principles & Practices*. Prentice Hall International Inc., New Jersey, third edition, 2000.

207. C. C. Walker. Behavior of a class of complex systems: the effect of system size on properties of terminal cycles. *Journal of Cybernetics*, 1(4):55–67, 1971.

208. C. C. Walker. Attractor dominance patterns in sparsely connected boolean nets. *Physica D*, 45:441–451, 1990.

209. D. Wang. Temporal Pattern Processing. In Arbib [10].

210. X. Wang and E. K. Blum. Dynamics and bifurcation of neural networks. In Arbib [10], pages 339–343.

211. P. Wegner. Interactive foundations of computing. *Theorectical Computer Science*, 192:315–351, 1998.

212. G. Weisbuch. *Dynamique des systèmes complexes: Une introduction aux réseaux d'automates*. InterEditions, France, 1989.

213. G. Weisbuch. *Complex Systems Dynamics: An Introduction to Automata Networks*, volume 2 of *Lecture Notes, Santa Fe Institute, Studies in the Sciences of Complexity*. Addison-Wesley, Redwood City, CA, 1991.

214. D. Welsh. *Codes and Cryptography*. Oxford University Press, New York, 1988.

215. N. Wiener. *Cybernetics or Control and Communication in the Animal and Machine*. MIT Press, Cambridge, MA, 1948.

216. Xilinx. *Virtex 2.5V Field Programmable Gate Arrays, Advanced Product Specification*, February 1999. http://www.xilinx.com.

217. X. Yao. Evolving Artificial Neural Networks. *Proceedings of the IEEE*, 87(9):1423–1447, September 1999.

218. X. Yao and Y. Liu. Evolving artificial neural networks through evolutionary programming. In *Fifth Annual Conference on Evolutionary Programming*, pages 257–266, San Diego, CA, 2 March 1996. MIT Press.

219. X. Yao and Y. Liu. A New Evolutionary System for Evolving Artificial Neural Networks. *IEEE Transactions on Neural Networks*, 8(3):694–713, 1997.

220. M. J. Zigmond, F. E. Bloom, S. C. Landis, J. L. Roberts, and L. R. Squire, editors. *Fundamental Neuroscience*. Academic Press, San Diego, CA, 1999.

221. K. G. Zipf. *Human Behavior and the Principle of Least Effort*. Addison-Wesley, Cambridge, MA, 1949.

Index